IRAQ
in Pictures

Stacy Taus-Bolstad

Lerner Publications Company

Contents

Lerner Publications Company
A division of Lerner Publishing Group
241 First Avenue North
Minneapolis, MN 55401 U.S.A.

Website address: www.lernerbooks.com

Library of Congress Cataloging-in-Publication Data

Taus-Bolstad, Stacy.
    Iraq in pictures / by Stacy Taus-Bolstad.— Rev. and expanded.
        p.   cm. — (Visual geography series)
    Includes bibliographical references and index.
    Summary: Introduces the land, history, government, culture, people, and economy of Iraq.
    ISBN: 0-8225-0934-2 (lib. bdg. : alk. paper)
    1. Iraq—Juvenile literature. 2. Iraq—Pictorial works—Juvenile literature. [1. Iraq.] I. Title. II. Visual
geography series (Minneapolis, Minn.)
DS70.62.T38 2004
956.7—dc21   2003005627

Manufactured in the United States of America
1 2 3 4 5 6 - JR - 09 08 07 06 05 04

INTRODUCTION

The early twenty-first century brought a U.S.-led war to Iraq that toppled the controversial dictator Saddam Hussein and left the nation struggling toward democracy. But even before the war, tensions had been high between Iraq and the United States. In August 1990, Saddam Hussein had ordered the invasion of neighboring Kuwait, an act that provoked the military response of the United States along with forces from many countries. Called the Persian Gulf War, or Gulf War, the conflict ended in a defeated Iraq and the deaths of thousands of Iraqi soldiers and civilians. After the Gulf War, a cease-fire agreement seemed to have resolved the conflict.

But Hussein soon made international headlines again by refusing to comply with the terms of the cease-fire. Throughout the 1990s, the United Nations (UN) regarded Iraq and its weapons programs as a threat to world peace. In 2001, after Islamic terrorists bombed New York City's World Trade Center and Washington, D.C.'s Pentagon, the United States turned a suspicious eye on Iraq. Although no known link between the terrorist attacks and Saddam Hussein appeared, U.S.

president George W. Bush declared Iraq to be a member of the so-called "Axis of Evil" along with Iran and North Korea. Bush claimed that these countries had dangerous governments and probably possessed weapons of mass destruction.

In September 2002, President Bush addressed world leaders gathered at a UN General Assembly session in New York and expressed his desire to confront the "grave and gathering danger" of Iraq. Many countries, including France and Germany, were skeptical of the immediate threat posed by Iraq. But in November 2002, UN weapons inspectors entered the country, backed by a UN resolution that threatened "serious conse-quences" if Iraq was found to be in breach of its weapons agreement. No weapons of mass destruction were found, but President Bush asserted that the Iraqi government was not cooperating with inspectors.

In the spring of 2003, President Bush and British prime minister Tony Blair mobilized their forces. On March 17, President Bush gave Hussein and his sons forty-eight hours to leave Iraq or face war.

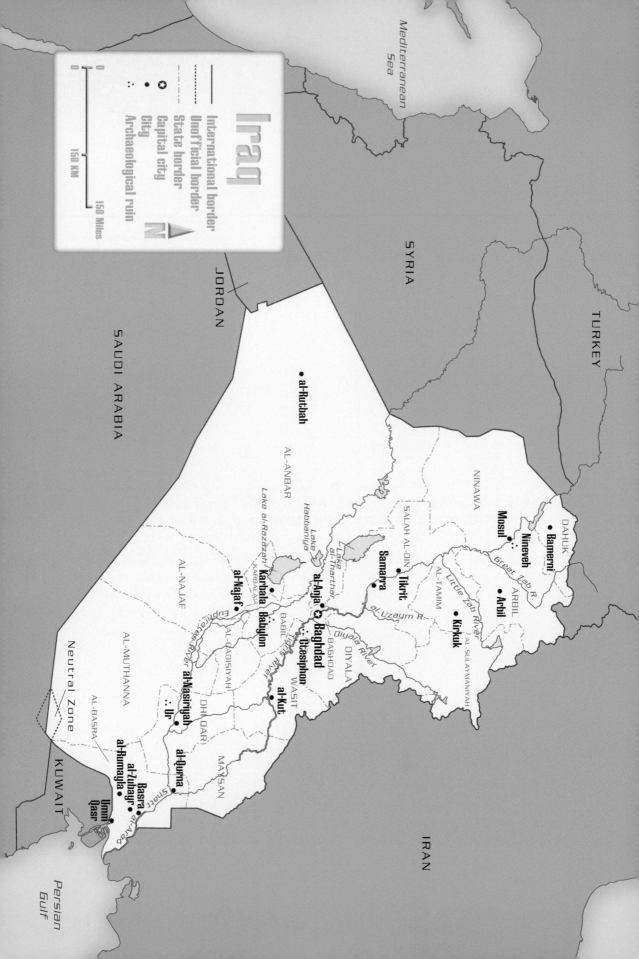

Mediterranean Sea

SYRIA

TURKEY

JORDAN

SAUDI ARABIA

Iraq

International border
Unofficial border
State border
Capital city
City
Archaeological ruin

N

150 KM   150 Miles

• al-Rutbah

AL-ANBAR

Lake al-Razazah
Lake Habbaniya
Lake al-Tharthar

NINAWA

Mosul •
Nineveh ∴
⦿ Bamerni

DAHUK

Great Zab R.

SALAH AL-DIN

Samarra •
Tikrit •

• Arbil

ARBIL

Little Zab River

AL-TAMIM

• Kirkuk

AL-SULAYMANIYYAH

al-Najaf •
Karbala
KARBALA

al-Anja •

Babylon
BABIL

al-Uzaym R.

⦿ Baghdad
Ctesiphon

BAGHDAD

Diyala River

DIYALA

TIGRIS RIVER

Euphrates River

AL-QADISIYAH

AL-NAJAF

AL-MUTHANNA

Neutral Zone

AL-BASRA

al-Nasiriyah •
∴ Ur

DHI QAR

WASIT

• al-Kut

MAYSAN

IRAN

al-Qurna •

Basra
al-Zubayr •
al-Rumayla •

Shatt al-Arab

KUWAIT

Umm Qasr •

Persian Gulf

Beginning on March 20, 2003, U.S. bombs exploded across the Iraqi capital of Baghdad, leaving targeted buildings in ruins. In southern Iraq, near the city of Basra, U.S. and British troops clashed with Iraqi soldiers. The attacks signaled the beginning of a U.S.-led military operation to remove Saddam Hussein from power and to establish a new political order in Iraq. When the attacks ended on April 15, 2003, Hussein and his sons were missing, and U.S. troops held Baghdad.

Many Iraqis welcomed the occupying U.S. soldiers, but others erupted in protest. Stores and hospitals were looted, museums were vandalized, and civilians were killed in protest-related violence. Groups of Iraqis, some apparently loyal to Hussein and others who want foreign troops out of Iraq, have continued to attack and sabotage U.S.-led coalition targets, as well as UN and civilian sites, in Iraq. A suicide bombing of UN headquarters in Baghdad and sabotage of oil pipelines and water mains in the summer of 2003 have proved devastating to the rebuilding of Iraq.

The postwar democratization of Iraq remains in the developmental stages. U.S. and coalition forces continue to seek out Saddam Hussein and ranking members of his government in an attempt to bring them to justice and to prevent their disruption of plans for a democratic government in Iraq. Several officials have been captured during raids. Hussein's sons, Uday and Qusay, were killed during a gunfight stemming from one such raid in July 2003. Taha Yassin Raman, former Iraqi vice president and top Hussein aide, was arrested in August 2003.

The U.S. government has assembled a team of civilian administrators, called the Governing Council, to oversee Iraq's transition to democratic government. The Governing Council began its first official meetings and took its first governing action in July 2003. But until the rioting, sabotage, and ongoing fighting end, a stable political system may be difficult to uphold. Time will tell if Iraq can recover from a debilitating war and emerge as a free and democratic nation.

Members of Iraq's temporary government, the Governing Council. Plans for postwar Iraq include free elections for a government chosen by the people.

THE LAND

Located at the northern end of the Persian Gulf, Iraq covers an area of about 169,236 square miles (438,319 square kilometers). The nation is slightly larger than the state of California. Turkey and Syria border Iraq to the north and northwest, and Jordan lies to the west. Iran is Iraq's eastern neighbor, and Kuwait and Saudi Arabia are located to the south. The southeastern corner of Iraq touches the Persian Gulf.

Boundary disputes between Iraq and some of its neighbors—particularly Iran and Kuwait—have been an ongoing source of tension and conflict. Iraq's border with Iran was originally established in a 1937 treaty that divided the channel called the Shatt al-Arab between them. But Iran and Iraq both disagreed about the actual boundary. In 1975 the two countries agreed to define the common border as the entire length of the Shatt al-Arab estuary—the spot where the waterway flows into the gulf. Because the new boundary resulted in a loss of land for Iraq, pockets of territory along the mountain border were designated as Iraqi. Nevertheless, in the 1980s, the two countries went to war over the disputed boundary.

Iraq's boundary with Kuwait has also presented problems. In the last decades of the twentieth century, Iraq argued that the border, originally set in a 1913 treaty, was unacceptable. It claimed that parts of Kuwait, including some of Kuwait's rich oil fields, should belong to Iraq.

Topography

Iraq has three main topographical regions. Mountains separate the northeastern part of Iraq from Iran, and a wide, flat plain lies in the center of the country. Deserts are located in the west and southwest.

The Zagros Mountains rise in northeastern Iraq and extend into Iran. This range has many peaks above 9,000 feet (2,743 meters) and some above 10,000 feet (3,048 m) near Iraq's borders with Turkey and Iran. Two of Iraq's highest summits are Haji Ibrahim at 11,811 feet (3,600 m) and Sar-i Kurawah at 10,991 feet (3,350 m). The foothills and valleys of the Zagros Mountains are home to most of Iraq's Kurdish people.

Iraqi Kurds form a strong minority of the population. The region also contains some of Iraq's richest mineral deposits.

The plain is divided into upper and lower sections. The Upper Plain begins northwest of the city of Samarra between the Tigris and Euphrates Rivers and extends into Turkey and Syria. Hills in the region reach heights of 1,000 feet (305 m) above sea level, and rolling grasslands are common. Deep valleys cut through the Upper Plain, though higher areas remain dry and hard to irrigate.

The Lower Plain reaches south from Samarra to the Persian Gulf. This part of the plain is alluvial—that is, it consists of a mixture of clay, sand, rocks, and silt that have been deposited through centuries of flooding. The Lower Plain includes a delta (a fertile triangular area) at the mouths of the Tigris and Euphrates. Most of the country's people live in this region. Just south of the delta—near the city of al-Qurna—the land becomes marshy. The Madan, or Marsh Arabs, inhabit the swampland, living in arched dwellings built of reeds.

Western Iraq holds a section of the Syrian Desert, which stretches into Syria, Jordan, and Saudi Arabia. In the southwest is another desert, al-Hajara, which extends into Saudi Arabia. The nation's hot zones—which are flat, rocky, and sparsely vegetated—contain several wadis (dry riverbeds). When seasonal rains come, these wadis can fill up with water, often causing short but devastating floods. Some wadis run more than 250 miles (400 km) long.

Al-Hajara is home to many desert clans such as the Bedouin. At the southern edge of al-Hajara is the diamond-shaped Neutral Zone.

The Zagros Mountains rise up from a valley in northeastern Iraq. The region is home to Iraqi Kurds.

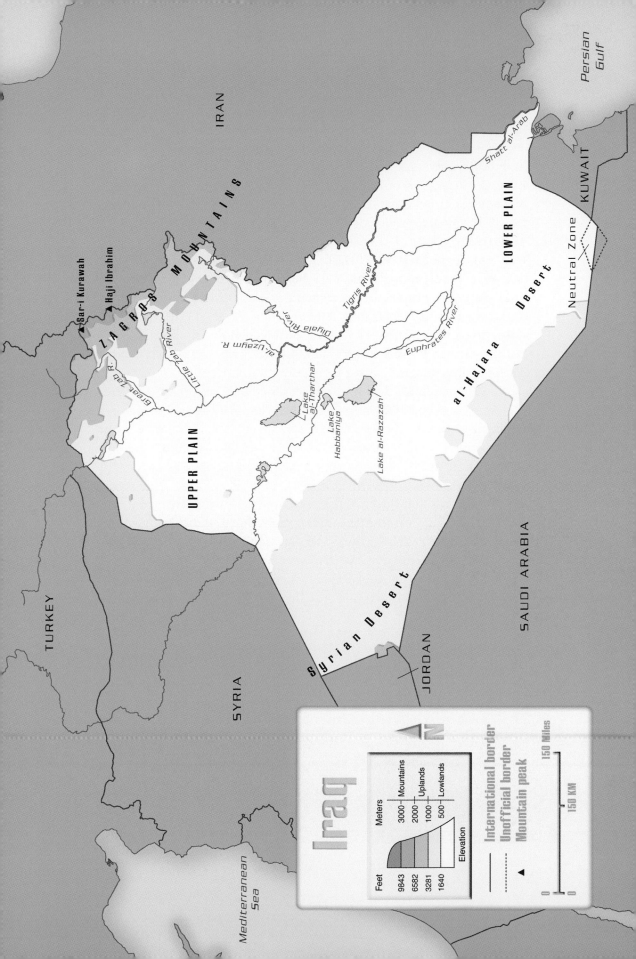

Mediterranean
Sea

TURKEY

SYRIA

IRAN

ZAGROS
MOUNTAINS

Sar-i Kurawah
Haji Ibrahim

Great Zab R.
Little Zab River
al-Uzaym R.
Diyala River
Tigris River
Euphrates River

Shatt al-Arab

Persian
Gulf

KUWAIT

LOWER PLAIN

Neutral Zone

UPPER PLAIN

Lake
al-Tharthar
Lake
Habbaniya
Lake al-Razazah

al-Hajara
Desert

Syrian Desert

JORDAN

SAUDI ARABIA

Iraq

N

Feet   Meters
9843
6582   3000 — Mountains
3281   2000 — Uplands
1640   1000 — Lowlands
            500
Elevation

International border
Unofficial border
▲ Mountain peak

0   150 KM   150 Miles

The Neutral Zone, first outlined in 1922, is a buffer between Iraq and Saudi Arabia. It allows the Bedouin, herders who move from place to place with their animals, to move freely between the two countries. The Neutral Zone's official boundaries were established by a treaty in 1975. Following a 1981 treaty, the zone was divided equally between the two countries, though it is still unofficially recognized for the sake of Bedouin migrations.

Rivers and Lakes

Iraq's two main rivers—the Tigris and the Euphrates—have carried fertile soil to nearby river valleys for centuries. The Tigris starts its 1,180-mile (1,899-km) course in Turkey's Lake Hazer and Lake Van. The Euphrates rises in eastern Turkey and has a total length of 1,820 miles (2,929 km). At the point where the rivers flow into Iraq, 25 miles (40 km) of open plain separate them from each other. The Tigris flows south, and the Euphrates takes a southeastern direction.

The Euphrates has no tributaries (other streams and rivers that feed into it) in Iraq. The Tigris, on the other hand, is fed by several waterways, including the Great Zab, Little Zab, Diyala, and al-Uzaym Rivers. Iraq has several lakes. The country's three main lakes all lie in the central part of the country. Lake al-Tharthar and Lake Habbaniya are west of Samarra and Baghdad. Lake al-Razazah is near Karbala.

At al-Qurna, the waters of the Tigris and the Euphrates combine to form the Shatt al-Arab. This 120-mile-long (193-km-long) channel connects the port of Basra with the Persian Gulf. Oceangoing vessels reach Basra by way of this broad waterway.

Iraq and its eastern neighbor, Iran, have long vied for control of the Shatt al-Arab. Part of the waterway flows between the two countries.

Fishers pull in their nets from the **Shatt al-Arab,** Iraq's only navigable link to the Persian Gulf. The country has fought to retain control of the waterway.

Arabian camels are native to Iraq. Their thick fur insulates them from extreme desert temperatures.

CAMELS

Camels are important to Iraq's desert people. Often called "ships of the desert," these pack animals are a perfect means of transportation across the country's barren landscape. Camels can go for long periods without water, and they live on desert plants. Their wide, flat feet are made for walking on the hot sand—when they step, the tough pads of their feet spread out to prevent them from sinking in the sand. Their eyes and nostrils can close against blowing sand. In addition, camels are a source of milk and meat for their owners. If you'd like to learn more about camels, go to vgsbooks.com

The area was heavily bombed in the Iran-Iraq War in the 1980s and during the Persian Gulf War in the 1990s. Iraq controls the entire channel, as well as the port of al-Faw, where the Shatt al-Arab enters the Persian Gulf. Abadan, Iran's major oil-refining city, lies along the waterway's banks.

Flora and Fauna

Little vegetation grows in Iraq because of its sparse rainfall. Reeds, box-thorns, buttercups, rushes, and saltbushes grow on the nation's plains and in marshlands. Date palms thrive in many parts of the country. Poplars and willows grow in some places. Rough, drought-resistant vegetation such as rockrose, storksbill, and catchfly cover desert areas. In the spring, when the rains come, these plants bloom and provide food for sheep, goats, and camels.

Iraq's mammals include bats, rats, jackals, hyenas, and wildcats, with wild pigs and gazelles living in remote areas. Reptiles are numerous. Lizards and snakes make their homes in the country's deserts. Among Iraq's domesticated animals are camels, oxen, water buffalo, and horses. These animals are tamed and can be used to help humans in farming and for transportation. Northern Iraqis raise large flocks of sheep and goats for their wool and skins.

> Want to learn more about Iraq's climate? Visit vgsbooks.com for a link to information about what the weather is like in Iraq right now.

Iraq's game birds include wild ducks, geese, black partridges, bustards, and sandgrouse. Birds of prey—such as falcons, eagles, hawks, and buzzards—feed on small mammals. The Tigris, the Euphrates, and the Shatt al-Arab contain freshwater fish, which are an important part of the Iraqi diet.

Climate

Iraq has two seasons—wet winters and dry summers. Summer runs from May to October, and winter lasts from November to April. The highest temperatures, which usually occur between June and September, exceed 100°F (38°C). Records show even hotter temperature readings—up to more than 120°F (49°C)—in regions along the Persian Gulf. Average summer temperatures in the deserts measure in the 90s°F (33°C–37°C). Mountain areas of Iraq are cool in summer, with sharp temperature drops at night.

Winters, although sometimes cold, are generally mild and sunny. In central Iraq, average winter temperatures hover around 40°F (4°C) and drop to about 30°F (–1°C) in the deserts. In the mountainous northeast, however, winter temperatures fall well below freezing and are usually accompanied by snow.

Iraq's average yearly rainfall is 5 inches (13 centimeters) in the deserts and 15 inches (38 cm) in the northern mountains. In the highest elevations of the northeast, yearly precipitation (rain and snow) of 40 inches (102 cm) is not uncommon, and snow frequently falls on the highest peaks. The deserts receive little rainfall.

Iraq has two wind patterns. The eastern wind, called a *sharki*, is hot, dry, and dusty. Sharki winds blow from April to June and from September to November. Their strong gusts can reach 50 miles (80 km) per hour and often kick up huge walls of dust. The other pattern,

known as a *shamal*, is a steady, northern wind that brings some relief from the extreme heat of summer.

Natural Resources and Environmental Issues

In addition to its vast oil reserves, Iraq has deposits of sulfur, salt, coal, gypsum (used in making plaster), lead, and zinc. Aside from oil, however, these minerals are generally not mined in any great quantities.

One of the leading oil-producing countries of the world, Iraq contains large reserves of oil. Primary oil fields lie near Kirkuk between the Zagros Mountains and the Upper Plain, in the al-Zubayr–al-Rumayla region west of Basra, and near the city of Mosul.

Damage from the 2003 war, added to that from the 1991 Gulf War, have created numerous environmental emergencies in the country. The lack of electricity has caused water pumps to malfunction throughout Iraq. Without fresh water, desperate Iraqis have broken underground pipes and have become sick from the unsanitary water inside.

Iraqi soldiers burned oil fields in Rumaila and other areas of southern Iraq during the 2003 war to keep the United States from seizing working wells. Burning oil fields have poisoned the air with sulfur dioxide and other dangerous pollutants.

Tank-busting shells containing depleted uranium (DU) were used in the Gulf War and in the 2003 war and have been confirmed as sources of dangerous radioactive dust. This radioactive substance can attack the kidneys if ingested or cause lung cancer if inhaled. The total DU contamination of Iraqi land and water has yet to be fully investigated, but the United Nations has urged that the substance be located and cleaned up as soon as possible.

Cities

BAGHDAD—the capital of Iraq—is located on both banks of the Tigris River. The city has traditionally been a center of trade, manufacturing, and culture.

Baghdad, Iraq's capital, sustained heavy bombing *(left)* during fighting in 2003. The ancient capital city has withstood a history of onslaught.

Before the 2003 war, the capital was home to more than 4.3 million people, most of whom are Muslims (followers of the Islamic religion). It is unknown how many civilians fled the city as the result of the 2003 conflict, but estimates are in the thousands.

The center of Baghdad is made up of two districts, a modern section on the west bank of the Tigris and an ancient section on the east bank. The old part of the city—with its narrow streets and noisy bazaars (open-air markets)—has been inhabited for centuries. In recent years, modern structures, which include hotels and banks, were built in the center of the city. After the mass U.S. bombings of the city in 2003, however, Baghdad's infrastructure lay in ruins. In addition to the destruction of many government buildings, electricity and telephone services were downed throughout the city. Saboteurs blew up a major water main in the city, temporarily cutting off much needed water supplies to Baghdad residents. Rebuilding Baghdad is one of Iraq's biggest priorities in the wake of the conflict.

BASRA (population 1.5 million prior to the 2003 war) is Iraq's chief port, although it lies 75 miles (121 km) from the Persian Gulf. Oceangoing vessels travel up and down the Shatt al-Arab to the city's port. The city's southern location at the head of the Shatt al-Arab made it a target for bombing raids during the Iran-Iraq War, the Persian Gulf War, and the 2003 war. The bombings seriously damaged Basra's oil plants, and much of the population left the city. After the 2003 conflict, the city experienced looting and an outbreak of cholera, caused by contaminated water.

British troops, part of the coalition forces, occupy Basra during the 2003 conflict in Iraq. Founded in the seventh century A.D., Basra has historically been of strategic military importance as a major seaport in the region.

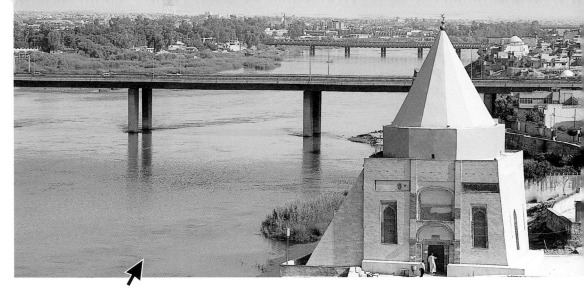

The city of **Mosul** lies across from the ancient ruins of Nineveh on the Tigris River. Mosul became a major trade center in the eighth century A.D. because of its location along a caravan (trade) route between India and Persia (modern-day Iran).

Basra contains the facilities, however—including an airport, railways, and several refining complexes—to regain its former commercial position.

MOSUL, the main city of northern Iraq, is situated on the west bank of the Tigris. Since the 1930s, Mosul has owed its prosperity to the oil fields of the surrounding countryside. Before that time, cotton weaving was the city's chief source of income. Centuries ago, Mosul was famous for its fine cotton cloth (called muslin), and weaving is still an important industry for the city. The city also trades locally produced wool, animal hides, and nuts.

While most of Mosul's nearly 1.2 million residents are Muslims, large numbers of Christians also live in the region. As a result, Christian and Muslim holy places stand side by side in the city. Adding to the area's historical interest are the ruins of Nineveh—the ancient capital of the Assyrian Empire—which lie across the Tigris from Mosul. Mosul was a hot spot of anti-Western protest following the 2003 war and the city in which coalition forces found Saddam Hussein's sons and the former Iraqi vice president.

KIRKUK (population 535,000), in northeastern Iraq, is another city built on oil profits. The city was once a center for agricultural products such as fruits and grains, but modern Kirkuk has become an important petroleum hub. Several oil pipelines begin at Kirkuk and run westward through Syria, Lebanon, and Turkey to ports on the Mediterranean coast. The oil fields in Kirkuk are an important source of income for Iraq's postwar reconstruction, though the region's pipelines have been the target of sabotage, which threatens oil distribution to lucrative world markets.

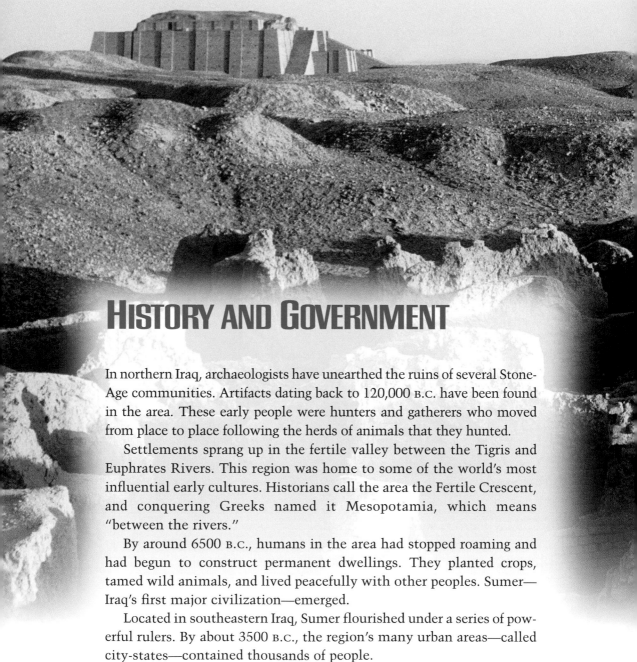

HISTORY AND GOVERNMENT

In northern Iraq, archaeologists have unearthed the ruins of several Stone-Age communities. Artifacts dating back to 120,000 B.C. have been found in the area. These early people were hunters and gatherers who moved from place to place following the herds of animals that they hunted.

Settlements sprang up in the fertile valley between the Tigris and Euphrates Rivers. This region was home to some of the world's most influential early cultures. Historians call the area the Fertile Crescent, and conquering Greeks named it Mesopotamia, which means "between the rivers."

By around 6500 B.C., humans in the area had stopped roaming and had begun to construct permanent dwellings. They planted crops, tamed wild animals, and lived peacefully with other peoples. Sumer—Iraq's first major civilization—emerged.

Located in southeastern Iraq, Sumer flourished under a series of powerful rulers. By about 3500 B.C., the region's many urban areas—called city-states—contained thousands of people.

Improved farming methods, such as the creation of the plow, fostered Sumer's wealth. Sumerian engineers built irrigation canals to control the unpredictable waters of the Tigris and Euphrates. The Sumerians also developed powerful weapons and made accurate measurements of time and area. Sumerian architects built huge temples, called ziggurats (such as the one at left), which were pyramids made of brick.

Sumer's leaders established trade routes to regions that would become modern-day Turkey and Iran. Merchants exchanged locally produced grain and cloth for foreign metals. The heavy trade demanded complex record keeping and thus may have encouraged the development of a writing system called cuneiform.

Sumer was not a unified nation. Each of its many city-states—including Ur, Erech, Eridu, Kish, and Laash—was powerful. The rulers of the city-states frequently warred with one another. In addition, other peoples in the region attacked the small realms.

Sumerians are given credit for inventing cuneiform (an early system of writing), sailboats, standardized weights, the lyre (a musical instrument), soap, farming tools such as the plow and sickle, and even board games. Find a variety of links at vgsbooks.com, where you can find out more about the Sumerians and the ancient civilizations of Mesopotamia.

Early Conquerors

In about 2300 B.C., Sargon of Akkad conquered various Sumerian city-states. Sargon and his people, called Akkadians, absorbed many Sumerian traditions and technology. But other local groups later replaced the Akkadians. Among the new-comers were the Amorites, a people originally from Syria, who founded their capital at Babylon in the northern part of the Lower Plain. Eventually called Babylonians, the new conquerors had gained complete control of the Tigris-Euphrates region by about 1800 B.C. One of the Babylonian kings, Hammurabi, united the city-states.

Hammurabi created one of the world's first complete collection of laws, called the Code of Hammurabi. Hammurabi's laws covered issues such as property rights, taxes, labor, and family affairs. The code was the foundation for many other judicial systems in the region.

Hammurabi (right) receives laws, called the **Code of Hammurabi,** from the Sun god, Shamash. Toward the end of his reign, King Hammurabi wanted his judgments to be carved on stone and placed in temples as proof that he had been a just ruler. The code is the most complete set of laws from ancient times.

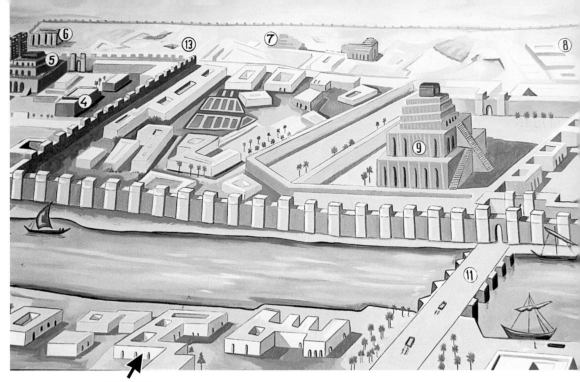

The city of **Babylon** as it might have looked under the reign of Chaldean king Nebuchadrezzar II. One of the king's grand temples stands at right.

After Hammurabi died in 1750 B.C., his empire crumbled. By 1600 B.C., the Hittites—a group based in Turkey—had plundered Babylonia, leaving it weak and unprotected. The Kassites, from the Zagros Mountains, seized control in about 1570 B.C. They ruled for the next four centuries. Although little is known about the Kassite period, it was a prosperous time for Babylonia.

In the thirteenth and twelfth centuries B.C., the entire area around the eastern Mediterranean Sea—including present-day Turkey, Syria, Jordan, and Iraq—experienced a period of severe upheaval. In 1150 B.C., invading Elamites from the east removed the Kassite ruler and destroyed the capital. For several centuries, Babylonia grew weak under a series of rulers who could not unite the population.

▷ Foreign Invaders

The Assyrians, who lived north of the Tigris-Euphrates plain, began to rebuild their empire in the ninth century B.C. Their realm soon stretched from the Mediterranean coast to modern northwest Iran.

But the Assyrians faced many rebellions among conquered peoples. By 612 B.C., revolts by the Chaldeans—people who inhabited the marshlands of southern Sumer—had toppled the Assyrians. The Chaldeans then took control of Babylonia.

Perhaps the most famous Chaldean king was Nebuchadrezzar II, who reigned from 605 to 562 B.C. Nebuchadrezzar ordered the construction of magnificent palaces and tall temples within Babylon's city wall.

According to legend, Nebuchadrezzar II built the Hanging Gardens of Babylon for his new bride, Amytis. A Median princess, Amytis was homesick for her lush homeland. So Nebuchadrezzar ordered the building of a palace with a magnificent garden to ease her grief. The gardens consisted of a series of terraces, resembling a small mountain, filled with trees and plants. The gardens soon became famous as one of the Seven Wonders of the Ancient World.

Above the royal palace were the king's gardens—called the Hanging Gardens of Babylon. Rising 300 feet (91 m) above another section of the city was a tower (sometimes called the Tower of Babel) dedicated to the god Marduk.

Despite these feats, Babylonia remained an unstable state. Clashes between the royal family and religious leaders weakened the realm. By 539 B.C., the Achaemenids from neighboring Persia (modern Iran) had conquered Babylonia. Their leader was Cyrus. The Babylonians frequently rebelled, but the area remained in Persian hands until 331 B.C. In that year, the young Greek general Alexander the Great and his troops marched into Babylonia. The Babylonians welcomed the Greeks as liberators from Persian control.

Alexander had bold plans for his empire, which was to be centered in Babylon, but he died in 323 B.C., before his plans could be carried out. Power fell to Alexander's generals. Seleucus, head of Alexander's Greek cavalry, took over the area. He founded the Seleucid dynasty (family of rulers), which eventually ruled a large portion of the Middle East.

Under the Greeks, the city of Babylon lost its prominence, but it remained a stop on major trade routes. In addition, Greek scholars studied ancient Sumerian texts on astronomy and mathematics.

Seleucid control lasted for about two centuries. By 122 B.C., the Parthians, nomads from central Asia, had captured the region, which the Greeks called Mesopotamia. A few centuries later, another Persian dynasty, the Sassanians, dislodged the Parthians. By A.D. 227, Sassanian occupation was complete. The Sassanians would control the area for four hundred years.

Arrival of the Arabs

The Arabs—a group of people originating in the Arabian Peninsula and speaking the Arabic language—conquered the Persians in A.D. 637, bringing the end of Sassanian rule in Mesopotamia. A collection of rival clans, the Arabs had unified under the banner of Islam. The prophet Muhammad had founded Islam in Saudi Arabia in the early seventh century A.D. Islam required its followers to expand Islamic territory and to convert non-Islamic peoples. The Arab caliphs, Islamic religious and political leaders, soon converted the people of Mesopotamia to Islam.

Early in the history of Islam, an important religious split occurred. The disagreement concerned the method of choosing the next caliph. People who favored an elected leader came to be called Sunni Muslims. Others believed that only direct descendants of Muhammad should be caliphs. These people were called Shiite Muslims.

By about 665, the Sunnis controlled Mesopotamia under the Umayyad dynasty. But internal struggles and Shiite rebellions brought down the Umayyad clan, and rival Sunnis of the Abbasid dynasty took control in 750. The second Abbasid caliph, Abu Jafar al-Mansur, founded the city of Baghdad in 762, making it the capital of his realm.

The adoption of Islam brought great cultural and commercial rewards to Mesopotamia. The city of Baghdad grew in population and importance. Mathematicians invented Arabic numerals and a decimal system. Engineers improved the city's irrigation system.

The Abbasid dynasty sent ambassadors to many lands, including China and India. The dynasty conducted trade on an enormous scale, and Baghdad became a trading center for a wide variety of goods.

The Abbasid dynasty peaked in the ninth century. Between the tenth century and the twelfth century, however, the dynasty's control weakened. Other Islamic groups absorbed pieces of the empire.

Haroun al-Raschid, caliph of Baghdad from A.D. 786 to 809. Al-Raschid is considered one of the greatest Abbasid leaders. A glimpse of the grandeur of Baghdad under his rule is evident in the background.

Within Mesopotamia, caliphs became unifying political symbols but had little real authority. Mamluks, former slaves trained as warriors and who took control of Egypt and beyond, governed the region in the tenth century. A Shiite military faction held power in the eleventh century, and Sunni Turks ruled in the twelfth century. These various governments suffered from internal rivalries and frequent invasions. Mesopotamia's instability made it easy prey for a new force in world conquest—the Mongols.

Mongol and Ottoman Control

Originating in central Asia, the Mongols swept through most of ancient Asia and the Middle East. Under their leader Hulegu, the Mongols seized Baghdad in 1258. Baghdad lay in ruins, and Mesopotamia became a neglected province of a vast foreign empire. The area remained economically depressed and culturally poor for several centuries.

The Mongols did little to unify their realm, and it eventually split into smaller sections ruled by local leaders. In 1401 another Mongol force sacked Baghdad and then left the area.

Throughout the fifteenth century, nomadic and settled peoples competed for control of Mesopotamia. In 1509 Persian troops invaded Mesopotamia. They continued to harass the region until the Ottoman Empire, centered in present-day Turkey, took control of the area.

Suleyman ruled the Ottoman Empire from 1520 to 1566. A just lawgiver and brilliant military strategist, he was known by Ottomans as "Suleyman the Just." Those he conquered called him **"Suleyman the Magnificent."** Mesopotamians learned of Suleyman's might when he conquered Baghdad in 1535.

In 1535 the Ottoman sultan (emperor) Suleyman the Magnificent conquered Baghdad, and Mesopotamia began its 380-year history as part of the Ottoman Empire.

During the period of Ottoman control, Mesopotamia was divided into three provinces—Basra, Baghdad, and Mosul. Each had its own regional problems, such as conflicts between Shiite and Sunni factions, between Kurdish and Arab populations, and between Muslim and Christian groups.

Between the sixteenth century and the eighteenth century, Mesopotamia slowly declined. Corrupt administrators, famine, and foreign invasions further devastated the region. Yet the area's location and promise of wealth eventually attracted a new group of foreigners—the Europeans.

European Influence and World War I

European nations had traded with Mesopotamia for centuries, but frequent contact did not occur until the early nineteenth century. Two European powers, Germany and Great Britain, became interested in Mesopotamia. Germany wanted to strengthen its commercial link to the Middle East. In 1899 the Ottoman rulers agreed to let the Germans construct railroad lines from Konya, Turkey, to the city of Baghdad.

The British wanted to prevent German expansion in the area, which they feared might threaten communication and trade with India, a British-controlled nation. The British made alliances with other European powers and with local Islamic leaders to curb Germany's influence. In addition, Britain had become aware of the untapped oil wealth of the Middle East and sought to take control of this oil. The foreign interferences of Britain and Germany sparked several Arab independence movements in the early twentieth century. Arab nationalists sought greater self-rule for Arab populations throughout the Middle East.

World War I broke out in 1914, just when Arab independence movements were gaining momentum. The conflict pitted the Central Powers—including Germany, Austria, and the Ottoman Empire—against the Allies, led by France and Great Britain. Many Arab leaders promised to aid Britain by revolting against the Ottoman Turks. The British put a new king in charge. This king, Ibn Hussein, came from a prominent Arabian family descended from the prophet Muhammad.

In exchange for Arab cooperation, Britain agreed to recognize Arab independence after the war. Hussein and his sons, notably Prince Faisal, envisioned a single independent Arab kingdom. They sent their best soldiers to fight alongside the British against the Ottomans.

British troops occupied Basra in 1915, and they had control of Baghdad by 1917. A year later, the British forces headed north, taking Mosul in October 1918. By the end of the war, the British held all of Mesopotamia.

At the postwar peace conferences, Arab leaders expected to work out the details of Arab independence. But in 1920, the League of Nations put much of the Middle East under British administration. This arrangement, called a mandate, meant that Britain would establish responsible Arab governments in Middle Eastern nations according to a league-approved timetable. To many Arabs, being a mandated territory was the same as being a colony—a state separate from but ruled by another nation.

The failure of the British to fulfill their promises of independence encouraged Arab nationalism. Secret anti-British societies formed in Mesopotamia, and riots broke out in 1920.

The Kingdom of Iraq

Aided by British advisers, the Mesopotamians established a constitutional monarchy, called the Kingdom of Iraq. Iraq comes from an Arabic word meaning "the cliffs." A king would head the state. The government would consist of a council of ministers, or a cabinet, chosen from an elected legislature. The British asked Prince Faisal to be Iraq's first king, and a nationwide vote confirmed the choice. It was clear, however, that King Faisal I owed his throne to the British.

An **early Iraqi oil well** about 1920. British attempts to control the oil supply in the Kingdom of Iraq sparked tensions between Britain and the kingdom.

But Iraq was still a British mandate. In 1922 Britain signed a treaty with Iraq that promised complete independence to the new kingdom within ten years. The arrangement displeased some of Iraq's ethnic and religious groups—notably the Kurds of the north and the Shiite Muslims of the Euphrates River Valley. These groups were not well represented in the nation's new assembly. Both factions wanted to separate their lands from the rest of Iraq. Because of the resulting violence and unrest, Britain decided to maintain a military force in the country.

King Faisal I

The mandate period brought many improvements to Iraq. With British help, the new nation built schools and medical clinics and updated railways and port facilities. Irrigation systems were repaired, and new industries received government funding. The Iraqis improved the long-used Ottoman tax system and revised the national legal code.

The most important change came with the discovery of huge oil fields near Kirkuk in 1927. The Iraqi government allowed the Iraq Petroleum Company (IPC)—a British-dominated, multinational firm—to explore the region for oil. The company drilled for oil and built pipelines that stretched westward to ports on the Mediterranean Sea.

⊙ Independence and World War II

British control of Iraq ended in 1931, and Iraq became independent in 1932. The nation still had strong ties to Great Britain, however. To protect its growing oil interests in the Middle East, Britain kept military posts and personnel in Iraq.

Within a year of Iraq's independence, King Faisal died. His death unleashed conflicts that had been brewing for several years. The Shiites still feared the domination of the Sunnis, who occupied most government posts. The Kurds strongly favored separation from the rest of Iraq and asserted their claim to their own nation, called Kurdistan. The Assyrians—a Christian, pro-British group in northeastern Iraq—voiced a similar demand.

Faisal's son and successor, Ghazi, was unable to balance conflicting religious and ethnic demands. In addition, the Iraqi army entered the political arena and used its power to dismiss several cabinets in the 1930s and 1940s.

Amid this instability, King Ghazi died in an automobile accident in 1939. Faisal's three-year-old grandson, Faisal II, inherited the throne. Because Faisal II was a child, the young king's cousin, Prince Abd al-Ilah, ruled in his place. Within months of Ghazi's death, World War II (1939–1945) broke out. The Iraqi prime minister, Nuri al-Said, favored the British during the global conflict. But widespread anti-British feelings remained in the nation. Rashid Ali al-Kaylani, who replaced al-Said as prime minister in a cabinet shuffle in 1941, shared these sentiments.

To release Iraq from British domination, al-Kaylani allied himself with Germany, Britain's enemy. When the British asked permission to land some soldiers in Iraq in April 1941, the Iraqi government did not fully cooperate. In response, the British sent troops to Basra, where they clashed with the Iraqi army. By the end of May, the British had the upper hand, and the prime minister fled to Egypt. A pro-British government was assembled, and Iraq became a wartime base for British and U.S. forces stationed in the Middle East.

Revolution and Socialism

In 1945, the year the war ended, Iraq became a founding member of two important organizations. The Arab League formed in March to strengthen ties among Arab countries in the Middle East. In December Iraq also joined the United Nations.

In 1947 the UN split nearby Palestine into proposed Arab and Jewish states, a move that the Arab League strongly opposed. Following the creation of the Jewish state of Israel in 1948, members of the Arab League, including Iraq, sent troops to crush the new nation. Fighting lasted for several months, until the UN arranged a cease-fire. Iraq, however, remained opposed to a Jewish homeland in the Middle East. Most Iraqi Jews emigrated to Israel.

Oil and oil profits were among the major issues facing Iraq in the 1950s. After the Iraqis granted oil rights to foreigners, the petroleum industry flourished. But most of the money from oil ventures left the country. In the early 1950s, the Iraq Petroleum Company negotiated a new accord with Iraq. Under this arrangement, the nation obtained 50 percent of the company's oil profits, much of which was set aside for internal development. In an attempt to gain more bargaining power with foreign-owned oil companies, Iraq became a founding member of the Organization of Petroleum Exporting Countries (OPEC).

Although it gained some wealth in the 1950s, Iraq was still a poor nation. A wide gap existed between rich and poor and between pro-European and pro-Arab activists. The government, which was again

Colonel Abd al-Salam Arif (waving, right) addresses a group of supporters, explaining his plan for revolution and the overthrow of King Faisal II.

run by Nuri al-Said or his handpicked supporters, lobbied for aid from the United States and nations in Europe. Middle- and low-income groups were attracted by the growing pan-Arabic movement—an effort to politically and economically unite the nations of the Arab world.

Internal disagreements grew until 1958, when General Abdul Karim Kassem and Colonel Abd al-Salam Arif led a coup d'etat, a forceful, quick government takeover. During bloody fighting, al-Said, Prince Abd al-Ilah, and King Faisal II were killed. Following the coup, which Iraqis celebrate as the 1958 Revolution, Iraq declared itself a republic.

The leaders of the coup formed a new government, with Kassem as its head. But by the early 1960s, the Kassem regime had lost support. A military coup in 1963 deposed Kassem, who was later killed.

Members of the Syrian-based Baath Party had organized the overthrow, and one of the party's leaders, Ahmad Hasan al-Bakr, became prime minister. Abd al-Salam Arif was named president. Arif eventually forced al-Bakr from office, beginning a round of coups and countercoups that lasted through the 1960s.

In 1968 al-Bakr staged a final overthrow. Members of a remolded Baath Party assumed complete control of the government. In Iraq the

Baath Party's goal was to create a strong state that could influence other nations in the Middle East. Socialist principles, such as shared ownership of farms and industries and the elimination of economic inequalities, guided the new government. Chief among al-Bakr's colleagues was Saddam Hussein. Hussein became a key participant in the Revolutionary Command Council (RCC) that ran the country.

Iraq's oil industry underwent changes in the 1970s. In 1972 Iraq began to nationalize the IPC. That is, the company switched from private ownership to state control. The government set up the Iraqi National Oil Company to manage the country's entire oil industry.

Iran-Iraq War

Throughout the 1970s, the issue of Kurdistan—the self-governing nation proposed by the Kurds—sharply divided Iraq. The RCC agreed eventually to grant self-rule to the Kurds. Promises were broken, however, and Kurdish resentment grew. In 1974 Kurdish guerrillas, called the Pesh Merga, fought with Iraqi soldiers.

Iran, Iraq's neighbor and longtime adversary, sympathized with the Iraqi Kurds and sent them weapons. In 1975, however, Iran signed an agreement with Iraq, settling a boundary dispute over the Shatt al-Arab and cutting off aid to the Kurdish rebels. This move disabled the revolt, and by 1976 Kurdish resistance had ceased. During this period, Saddam Hussein's power grew within the Iraqi government. In 1979 Hussein pressured al-Bakr to resign. Saddam Hussein became president of Iraq, ruling as a violent dictator.

In 1980 Iraq demanded a revision of the 1975 Shatt al-Arab agreement, which Iran rejected. Iraqi forces invaded Iran that same year.

Centuries-old differences between Sunni and Shiite Muslims resurfaced. Although Sunnis dominated Iraq's power structure, the majority of Iraq's people were Shiites. Iran, a Shiite state, hoped that a call for Islamic unity would lead Iraqi Shiites to topple the nonreligious regime of Iraq. In addition, the Pesh Merga allied itself with Iran against Iraq in the war.

In the 1980s, thousands of Iranian and Iraqi civilians and soldiers were wounded, killed, or captured during the war. Basra suffered heavy casualties, and its port facilities were shut down. Iraq bombed Iran's oil facilities on the Persian Gulf. As a result of the destruction, the oil production of Iraq and Iran fell. The war limited the ability of both nations and neutral Arab states to ship oil through the Persian Gulf.

Most Arab countries supported Iraq. Clashes and counteroffensives occurred year after year. By the mid-1980s, the war had reached a stalemate, with neither side gaining new ground. The Arab League called for Iran and Iraq to agree to a UN-sponsored cease-fire. Iraq accepted the cease-fire in 1987, and Iran consented to it a year later.

urges Iraqi troops on to victory during the Iran-Iraq War. Religious tensions and disputes over the Shatt al-Arab touched off the war.

Soon after the cease-fire, the Iraqi army attacked Kurdish guerrillas who had sided with Iran. Kurdish villages were destroyed, and Iraqi troops even used outlawed poison gas to kill thousands of Kurdish civilians. Despite substantial evidence, Hussein denied that he had used poison gas against the Kurds.

The Gulf War and Its Aftermath

In August 1990, Iraqi forces attacked Kuwait and formally annexed the small oil-rich nation. The invasion followed a dispute between Iraq and Kuwait over oil, money, and land. Hussein charged that Kuwait had produced more than the agreed-upon amount of oil set by OPEC. Hussein believed that this overproduction by Kuwait drove down prices for oil, which decreased Iraq's oil income. Iraq also claimed that Kuwait had illegally tapped oil from an oil field on the Iraq-Kuwait border.

The UN condemned the attack and demanded that Hussein withdraw his troops from Kuwait. When Hussein refused, the UN imposed economic penalties, called sanctions, which cut off most international trade with Iraq, including the sale of oil. The invasion also involved a military response. Thirty-nine countries, led by the United States, participated in this defense—called Operation Desert Shield.

In November 1990, the UN authorized the use of military force to eject Iraqi troops if Iraq failed to withdraw by January 15, 1991. Iraq stood firm. It stationed hundreds of thousands of troops along its borders with Kuwait and Saudi Arabia. When the UN deadline passed, allied UN forces began an attack on Iraq known as Operation Desert Storm. Iraq responded by bombing sites in Saudi Arabia and Israel.

Burning oil wells in Kuwait, 1991. Retreating Iraqi troops set oil wells ablaze in an attempt to harm the Kuwaiti economy by stopping oil production.

The air war lasted forty-two days. It was followed by a one-hundred-hour ground war, which succeeded in forcing Iraq from Kuwait. The Iraqi army left Kuwait in ruins. It also damaged the environment by releasing oil into the Persian Gulf and by igniting Kuwait's oil fields. It took professional firefighters nine months to fully extinguish the burning oil wells. The war ended with a cease-fire agreement in February 1991.

But the violence did not end with the Gulf War. Two ethnic groups opposed to Hussein—Shiite Muslims in southern Iraq and Kurdish guerrillas in the north—began separate uprisings after the war. Hussein's army quickly stopped these rebellions, causing an estimated loss of 20,000 lives. Fearful of additional force by the Iraqi army, more than 1.5 million Kurds fled to Iraq's northern borders with Iran and Turkey.

The UN economic sanctions against Iraq continued throughout the 1990s. UN officials monitored economic activity within the country, including the production and exportation of oil. Cleanup and rebuilding of heavily bombed areas proceeded, but the country lacked resources and funds to adequately rebuild its factories and power plants. Unemployment soared.

In 1994 Iraq's troops again threatened Kuwait's border, forcing U.S. troops to again intervene. Iraq withdrew without confrontation. But in 1996, Hussein's troops fired at U.S. and allied patrol planes. Once again, the United States bombed Iraq.

Under the terms of the cease-fire, Iraq had agreed to allow UN inspectors to monitor and disarm its weapons plants. But Hussein was uncooperative, limiting access to these plants and intimidating inspectors. Hussein faced widespread international criticism.

The economic sanctions and the destruction caused by decades of war hurt the Iraqi people. The infant death rate skyrocketed, while the average life expectancy plummeted. In response to the suffering, the UN established the Oil-for-Food program in 1995, allowing Iraq to sell some of its oil in order to buy food and other necessities to aid Iraqi citizens.

Hussein forced his country into the world spotlight again in October 1997, when he openly defied weapons inspectors by denying them access to sites. He demanded that the UN remove Americans from the UN inspection team. The team suspended the inspections. In 1998 Hussein agreed to give inspectors unrestricted access to all suspected weapons sites. But by August of that year, he again refused to cooperate with the UN. This time, the United States and Great Britain took action by bombing weapons sites in a campaign called Operation Desert Fox.

The UN offered to lift economic sanctions if Iraq complied with weapons inspections for nine months. But Hussein refused and continued to keep inspectors at bay.

▶ September 11 and the 2003 War

On September 11, 2001, terrorists with links to Saudi Arabia and the Middle East attacked the World Trade Center in New York City and the Pentagon outside Washington, D.C. While Saddam Hussein was

George W. Bush

not believed to be linked to the action, he was the only Arab leader who did not express condolences for the attack, further raising tensions between Iraq and the United States.

By 2002 U.S. president George W. Bush was threatening military action unless weapons inspections continued. Under pressure, Iraq allowed inspectors back into the country in November 2002. They did not find any weapons of mass destruction during their stay, but some members of the inspection team felt they were not allowed total access to potential storage sites. In March 2003, chief weapons inspector, Hans Blix, reported that Iraqis were accelerating their cooperation, but inspectors needed more time to verify Iraq's compliance.

Saddam Hussein

Visit vgsbooks.com for the latest information and statistics regarding the 2003 war in Iraq. You'll find in-depth coverage of the conflict and current information on the status of the Iraqi government, including video clips, profiles, and more.

Blix's request for more time was denied. On March 17, the UN secretary-general ordered the evacuation of weapons inspectors from Iraq. The same day, Great Britain's ambassador to the UN announced that diplomacy with Iraq had come to an end.

President Bush brought together a coalition of allied countries, including Great Britain, Australia, and Poland. Coalition forces attacked Iraq on March 20, 2003. Titled Operation Iraqi Freedom, the attack was comprised of long-distance sea attacks, precise air strikes, and the advance of ground troops from southern Iraq through Baghdad to the north. The main objectives were to remove Saddam Hussein and the Baath Party from power, to seek out weapons of mass destruction, and to rebuild Iraq as a democratic country.

The first of these objectives was reached on April 9, 2003, when U.S.-led coalition forces poured into Baghdad. They seized the capital city and with it the political nerve center of Iraq. Although the city fell easily, the whereabouts of Saddam Hussein, his politically powerful sons, and weapons of mass destruction remained unknown. Nonetheless, the Baath Party was no longer in control, and as forces pushed north to secure the rest of the country, the United States began to plan for a postwar democratic Iraq.

A **terrorist bombing of UN headquarters in Baghdad** rocked the city on August 19, 2003, killing at least 17 people and injuring more than 100 others.

President Bush declared an end to major hostilities in Iraq on May 1, 2003, and the UN lifted economic sanctions. However, sabotage and pockets of fighting continue throughout the country. Many Iraqis have welcomed the fall of Hussein's brutal regime as well as the killing of his sons and the capture of the former Iraqi vice president in July and August 2003. But they also resent the power of the U.S. administrators who are overseeing the rule of the country until a permanent Iraqi government is in place. The people fear the emergence of a new dictator but know very little about the alternatives offered by capitalism and Western democracy.

Government

Before the 2003 war, Iraq was under the complete control of Saddam Hussein and his ten-member Revolutionary Command Council (RCC). The RCC was made up of the most elite members of the Baath Party. With Hussein ousted, his sons dead, and many of his closest aides captured, Iraq must work with U.S. civilian administrators.

Transition to a new government began on April 15, 2003, when Iraqi representatives met under the watchful eye of the U.S. administrators to discuss Iraq's political future. The group of representatives was comprised of Iraqi exiles and members of the country's main ethnic groups. Among the basic issues agreed upon at the meeting was the goal of a democratic future for postwar Iraq. The representatives also vowed to completely dissolve the Baath Party and to restore basic services to the region as soon as possible.

When Saddam Hussein was ousted from power in April 2003, his estimated wealth was between $10 and $20 billion. While in power, Hussein built more than one hundred luxury palaces all over Iraq for himself and for select members of his regime. Meanwhile, much of Iraq's population was living in severe poverty. Nearly one-third of Iraq's children were underweight.

President Bush has named Paul Bremer, a former head of counterterrorism at the U.S. State Department, to supervise Iraq's political and physical reconstruction. Working in conjunction with Bremer and other advisers, Iraq's interim government started meeting officially in July 2003. Local councils of Iraqi representatives also continue to meet, but the country still needs a constitution, a new judiciary, and a cabinet. President Bush has said he will only turn over Iraq's power to a democratically elected government. This has angered some Iraqi people who demand full control of their country. Bush has promised to work with Iraqi leaders to establish a constitution and freely held public elections.

THE PEOPLE

Iraq's population of 23.6 million people includes several ethnic groups. Arabs make up about 80 percent of the total population, and Kurds—the largest non-Arab group—compose about 15 percent of it. Small numbers of Turkomans, Assyrians, Armenians, and Iranians also live in Iraq.

Villages are spread evenly throughout the nation's river valleys. Most rural families farm for a living. Before the 2003 war, most farmers leased land from the Iraqi government.

Nomadic herders still roam the deserts and plains in search of food for their camels, sheep, and goats. These nomads live in round tents that they carry with them.

Nearly 70 percent of the country's population lives in cities. As more and more Iraqis move to urban areas, their numbers put pressure on housing, the job market, and basic services. The destruction of the 2003 war has led to even greater problems of overcrowding and pollution in most Iraqi cities.

Ethnic Groups

Iraq's largest minority group is the Kurds. These seminomads often farm or herd livestock to make a living. Although Kurds follow the Sunni sect of the Islamic religion, they have long fought against other Muslims to establish their own nation. Iraq's Kurds share ethnic ties with Kurds of Turkey, Iran, Syria, and some regions of the former Soviet Union. These ties have fueled the group's struggle for self-rule. Since the first Gulf War, around 4 million Kurds have lived in an autonomous region in northern Iraq, protected by U.S. and allied air patrols. The Kurds fought alongside U.S.-led coalition forces in the 2003 war and began to resettle into Iraqi lands after the war. It is unknown how the future Iraqi government will deal with this former opposition group.

Two minority groups—the Madan and the Bedouin—stand out among Iraq's Arabs. The Madan, who are also called Marsh Arabs, inhabit the swamplands near the mouth of the Shatt al-Arab. Most male Marsh Arabs are fishermen. Several families make up each Madan

Saddam Hussein's regime had a history of persecuting and even gassing the Kurds. During the 2003 war, the Kurds allied with U.S.-led coalition forces.In the aftermath of the war, the Kurds are pushing for a voice in the new Iraqi government. Like many former opposition groups, they are hoping for a form of self-governance with representatives in Baghdad to help decide on national issues.

village, and one dwelling is set aside for guests. Long, open boats take people across the watery landscape from house to house and from village to village. After the 2003 conflict, investigators reported that Hussein had killed up to 20 percent of the Madan people in confrontations that followed campaigns to drain marshes. The Baath regime drained marshes to create new farmland, forcing Marsh Arabs to relocate and change their lifestyle drastically. Madan men who protested were often shot by Iraqi soldiers.

Far from the water-based homes of the Madan are the lands of the Bedouin. Some Bedouins are desert wanderers who travel through the hot zones of the Middle East on a seasonal search for water and grass

 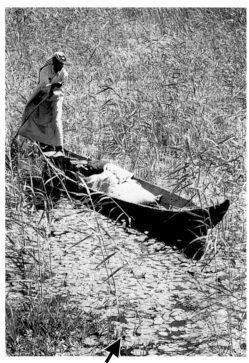

A **Kurdish man** *(left)* poses for the camera, and a **Madan man,** or Marsh Arab, navigates his longboat through marshland *(right)*.

A **Bedouin Arab herder** rests after finding grazing grounds for his camels. Kurdish, Madan, and Bedouin peoples make up Iraq's largest minority groups.

for their livestock. Iraq and Saudi Arabia each gave up a piece of their desert territory to form a neutral zone, which allows the Bedouin to move freely between the two countries. In recent years, however, many Bedouin have adopted more settled ways of life.

Traditionally, the Bedouin live in large woven tents. Each tent houses a family, and a group of related families makes up a clan. The Bedouin have a strong sense of family and clan loyalty. They are also famous for their courage and hospitality.

Smaller minority groups are scattered throughout Iraq. Assyrians live in the Zagros Mountains and near Mosul. Armenians have their own language and customs, and they have a strong trading community in Baghdad. Both the Assyrians and the Armenians belong to Christian sects.

Turkomans live in villages between Kirkuk and Mosul. Originally from the Ottoman Empire of Turkey, Iraq's Turkomans also share ethnic ties with peoples in the southern republics of the former Soviet Union. Because of the Iran-Iraq War, few people with Iranian backgrounds have remained in Iraq. Most of Iraq's Iranian people cluster near the holy cities of Karbala, al-Najaf, and Samarra.

Family Life and the Role of Women

In Iraq, family is the most important institution. It offers a strong support and social system. Each member of a family is responsible for maintaining the family's honor and for helping one another when necessary.

Extended family, which includes grandparents, aunts, uncles, and cousins, is just as important as immediate family. Individual status is generally determined by a person's position within his or her family and by the family's position in society.

Most Iraqi families are large, with an average of six children per Iraqi woman. Urban families are typically smaller than those living in the country. Iraqi children are taught to respect their elders. It is acceptable for extended family members and even neighbors to discipline a child. Young adults rarely live on their own. Most stay with their families until they are married.

Yet in Iraq, the birth of a son remains more celebrated than that of a daughter. One reason for this is that, as an adult, a son traditionally stays with the family and carries on the family's customs and name. He contributes to the family financially and also maintains its honor. A daughter, however, marries and becomes part of her husband's family.

Unrelated women and men are allowed to mingle in Iraq, though women are expected to be quiet and meek in the presence of men, particularly outside the home. However, within the home, women wield a great deal of power over their children and household affairs.

This group of **Iraqi women** from an extended family are shopping for clothing. The two daughters *(standing)*, mother *(sitting center)*, and aunt *(far right)* are wearing traditional and modern clothes.

Traditionally, Iraqi women did not work outside the home, but the recent wars have brought many women into the workforce, and they are playing a visible role in the rebuilding process in the wake of the 2003 conflict.

While many Iraqi women practice *hejab,* or modest dress, they are not required to. Most urban Iraqi women do not wear veils or full-length coverings, such as the chador, that are commonly seen in Islamic countries.

In the 1980s, the General Federation of Iraqi Women (GFIW) was founded to promote literacy and job training for women. Iraq also changed laws to limit discrimination against women in the workplace. The government passed laws to bring more equality for women in voting, divorce, and property ownership. Women's organizations in Iraq hope that social progress will come even faster when a democracy is established.

Health

Iraq had good medical facilities until the Gulf War in the 1990s. Until that time, government vaccination programs lowered the incidence of diseases such as diphtheria, tuberculosis, and measles. In addition, Iraqis received social benefits such as retirement pay, unemployment insurance, and sick leave. The government built new hospitals and encouraged people to study medicine by helping to pay for medical school.

Destruction from the Gulf War and the 2003 war negatively affected health conditions throughout Iraq. Heavy damage to water networks and sanitation systems, for example, left many people without access to clean water. Water pollution has increased cases of water-carried diseases, such as cholera, dysentery, and typhoid.

Economic sanctions and wartime destruction have led to decreased food supplies in Iraq. Although the government distributed food, most Iraqis, especially children, did not receive enough rations to meet recommended nutritional needs. Thousands of children died from malnourishment after the Gulf War, and many more were hospitalized with the condition.

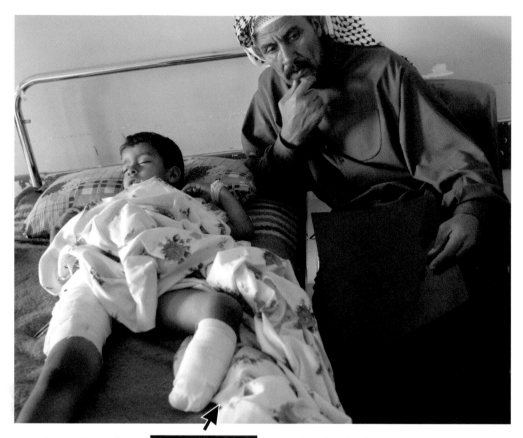

In an ill-equipped **Baghdad hospital,** an Iraqi father looks at an X ray of his injured son's leg. Since 1991, war and economic sanctions have strained and depleted Iraq's once remarkable health care system.

During the 2003 war, the country's most valuable health supplies were looted from the Ministry of Health. This made the treatment of war-related injuries very difficult. Those with life-threatening illnesses have struggled to find a place for their regular treatment. Important medicines are scarce, and power outages have made hospital equipment unreliable.

All of these factors have taken their toll on the general population. Life expectancy in Iraq is 56 years for men and 59 years for women. This is much lower than the Middle Eastern average of 68 years. For the region, the nation has a fairly high infant-mortality rate—103 deaths in every 1,000 live births—compared to the Middle Eastern average of 45 and the western European average of 5.

Education

Primary education in Iraq is mandatory and free. Schooling starts for children at age six and lasts for six years. Secondary education starts at age twelve and lasts for three to six years.

The country has nearly fifty teacher-training schools, nineteen technical colleges, and eight universities. In addition, Islamic universities—particularly those in al-Najaf and Karbala—are centers of religious education.

Education is less available for girls than for boys, as facilities for girls are more limited, and many rural and conservative families believe that women do not need education. Forty-six percent of Iraqi women can read and write, compared to 66 percent of adult Iraqi men. These averages are substantially lower than Middle Eastern literacy averages—68 percent for women and 86 percent for men.

While Iraq's educational system was once one of the best in the Arab world, war and economic sanctions have gravely damaged it. Schools lack supplies, such as books and teaching materials, and even water and electricity.

In the aftermath of the 2003 war, schools reopened with staggeringly low enrollment. A lack of teachers along with concerns about students' safety have kept many children in their homes. Primary school textbooks featuring quotes from Saddam Hussein are outdated.

These **Iraqi schoolchildren** took time to pose for the camera during recess at their school in Baghdad.

A significant part of Iraq's reconstruction is the task of creating an educational system to match developing governmental beliefs.

▷ Human Rights

Since 1968 Iraq's regime has been charged with multiple human rights abuses. Right up until the Baath Party collapsed in April 2003, the RCC's secret police force worked to repress antigovernment feelings and to keep the general population in line.

According to human rights groups such as Amnesty International and the Iraq Foundation, Iraqis who opposed Hussein and his administration—or those perceived to oppose the government—faced the threat of execution, torture, indefinite prison sentences, the loss of home and possessions, and deportation. Political rivals, ethnic and religious minorities, and even celebrities who became too popular were the target of these practices.

In the 1970s and 1980s, Hussein's regime deported an estimated 300,000 people, among them Kurds, Turkomans, and Shiites. Many Shiite religious scholars were believed to be executed at the same time.

A Shiite woman mourns the death of a family member at a **mass grave** in Iraq in 2003. As many as 15,000 people were buried at the site, victims of the Hussein government's retaliation against Shiites and Kurds in 1991.

If you would like to learn more about what is being done to improve conditions for the Iraqi people, go to vgsbooks.com for links to the Iraq Foundation, Human Rights Watch, and other human-rights organizations.

In 1991, following the Gulf War, Hussein retaliated against people and groups who had not supported his regime. The Kurds and Shiite Muslims were especially targeted, as many had openly rebelled during the war. An estimated two million Kurds, including children, fled into Turkey and Iran to avoid punishment.

Following the 2003 war in Iraq, human rights workers have been investigating newly discovered mass graves in southern Iraq. The shallow graves, found around Basra and al-Najaf, contain the bodies of Shiite Muslims. They supported an anti-Hussein religious leader who was assassinated in 1999. Human Rights Watch has estimated that the bodies of 200,000 people lie in unmarked graves in Iraq.

CULTURAL LIFE

Iraq's rich cultural life reflects the ancient Mesopotamian and Islamic influences that helped shape the modern nation. Ancient traditions in music, literature, weaving, painting, and carpet making have all survived the centuries and are practiced in modern Iraq. Ancient monuments stand proudly amid modern business offices, a reminder of the country's heritage.

◉ Religion

Religion is an important part of Iraqi cultural life. About 97 percent of Iraqis are Muslims. Fifty-seven percent of Iraqi Muslims belong to the Shiite sect, and 43 percent of Iraqi Muslims follow the Sunni sect.

Both sects accept the teachings of Muhammad, which are recorded in a book called the Quran. Sunni and Shiite Muslims have some very fundamental differences.

Shiites believe that Muhammad's closest male relative should have been his successor. This would have been his cousin and son-in-law

Ali Ibn Abi Talib. But Sunnis believe that his successor should be cho-sen from Muhammad's companions on the basis of wisdom and faith.

Sunnis and Shiites also differ in their attitudes toward Allah, the Arabic name for God. Sunni Muslims directly approach Allah through prayer. They believe that they do not need clergy or religious rites to speak to God. Shiites depend on imams—holy men who understand and follow the Quran—to be intermediaries between the faithful and Allah. For Sunni Muslims, an imam is one who leads other Muslims in prayer.

Regardless of the sect, Islam requires that its believers fulfill cer-tain obligations. Among these duties are daily prayer, fasting during the holy month of Ramadan, and making donations to the poor. In addition, Muslims must try to visit the holy city of Mecca in Saudi Arabia at least once in their lifetime.

A small percentage of Iraqis are Christians, and most belong to Catholic sects. The Assyrians are members of the Nestorian Church, a Christian sect that was founded in Iran in the fifth century A.D. Armenians make up a smaller proportion of Iraq's Christians. There are also minority communities of Syrian and Chaldean Catholics as well as a small population of Jews, most of whom live in Baghdad.

Religious Sites

Iraq contains several sites that have religious significance for the nation's Shiite Muslims. At al-Najaf in southern Iraq is a shrine to Ali Ibn Abi Talib—the seventh-century leader who founded the Shiite sect of the Islamic religion. Ali was assassinated in A.D. 661. Afterward, his followers honored him as a martyr to the Shiite cause.

Originally built in the late tenth century, Ali's tomb was subsequently sacked by foreign invaders. A new shrine replaced it in the sixteenth century. Each year, pilgrims from Iran, India, Pakistan, and Afghanistan visit al-Najaf to worship.

Thousands of Shiite Muslims also travel to Karbala on an annual pilgrimage. Located southwest of Baghdad, the city is the burial place of Husayn, a grandson of the prophet Muhammad. In A.D. 680, Husayn was killed in a revolt against the Sunnis. As a result, Shiites regard his tomb as a holy place and mark the date of his death with prayers of mourning. In 1991 Hussein's army severely damaged Karbala while stopping a Shiite uprising after the Persian Gulf War. The mass graves uncovered

Shiite Muslims make holy pilgrimages to the **shrine of Ali Ibn Abi Talib** at the center of al-Najaf. Thousands of pilgrims visit the site each year. Ali was the founder of the Shiite sect of Islam.

after the 2003 war are thought to be a consequence of this uprising, as many of the bodies are those of Shiite Muslims.

Language and Literature

The majority of Iraqis speak Arabic, the nation's official language and the main tongue of the Arab world. Written Arabic reads from right to left. Three forms of Arabic are used in Iraq. The Quran, the sacred book of Islamic writings, is written in classical Arabic. Almost any Arabic speaker can read modern standard Arabic, a later form of the language used mostly in writing. Iraqi Arabic, an Arabic dialect—a distinct version of the same language—is used in daily speech.

In addition to Arabic, most ethnic groups also speak their own language. The Assyrians speak Syriac, a language that evolved from an eastern Mesopotamian dialect. The Kurds use two Kurdish dialects, though written Kurdish uses the Arabic alphabet. English is also spoken, due to British influence.

> "I will proclaim to the world the deeds of Gilgamesh. This was the man to whom all things were known; this was the king who knew the countries of the world. He was wise, he saw mysteries and knew their secret things, and he brought us a tale of the days before the flood. He went on a long journey, was weary, worn-out with labor, returning he rested, he engraved on a stone the whole story."
>
> —from the *Epic of Gilgamesh*

Early Iraqi literature strongly influenced the writings of other cultures. The Christian Bible and sacred Jewish works share themes and subjects—such as the creation, the Garden of Eden, and the great flood—with ancient tales from Sumer, Babylonia, and Assyria. Among the most famous early epics (long narrative poems) is the Sumerian *Epic of Gilgamesh*. The story follows Gilgamesh, a legendary Sumerian king, in his search for eternal life.

This Chaldean stonework shows a scene from the *Epic of Gilgamesh*.

ARABIAN NIGHTS

The Thousand and One Nights, or *Arabian Nights*, are narrated by Scheherazade, a fictional princess whose husband, the king, threatens to kill her for betraying him. Scheherazade saves her life by telling her husband fanciful stories—and by not finishing each one until the next evening, at which time she starts a new story. After hearing the thousand and one stories, the king spares Scheherazade's life. From this collection come such tales as *Aladdin and the Magic Lamp* and the *Voyages of Sinbad the Sailor.*

The Arab conquest of the seventh century introduced vivid poetry and prose to the region, and these forms are still extremely popular in Iraq. Among the most famous folktales is *The Thousand and One Nights* (also known as *The Arabian Nights*). This collection of stories describes the adventures of fictional characters such as Aladdin and Sinbad.

Iraqi poetry and prose are meant to be recited, and skilled readers can draw attentive crowds at both private and public readings. Iraqi writers and playwrights also use other literary forms to express themselves, but the oral tradition reaches the largest public audience.

Arts and Architecture

The museums of Iraq, especially those in Baghdad, contain ancient artworks from many of Iraq's previous cultures. Carved slabs of stone, delicate jewelry, and fine textiles—as well as the unearthed remains of splendid ancient cities such as Nineveh—testify to the nation's long creative tradition.

In the first few days of the 2003 war, looters ransacked the Iraqi National Museum in Baghdad. Billions of dollars' worth of artifacts were stolen as gangs smuggled whatever they could from the museum. With help from coalition forces, the FBI (U.S. Federal Bureau of Investigation), Interpol (an international law enforcement organization), and UNESCO (United Nations Educational, Scientific, and Cultural Organization), some of the artifacts have been returned. While concerned Iraqis and UNESCO are striving to protect artifacts, the damage to Iraq's cultural history has been vast.

Iraq's architectural heritage stretches back to its ancient Sumerian settlements.

Gate of Nineveh

Remains of the **wall of Babylon** *(right)* still stand in Iraq. The gods Adad, represented as a bull *(top right)*, and Murduk represented as a dragon, *(bottom right)*, adorn this section of the wall. Built in the ninth century, Samarra's **spiral minaret (tower)** rises above the Great Mosque.

Ruins of palaces and cities are scattered throughout the country. Sumerian architecture, which was ornate and complex, often included clay as its principal building material. Imported stone and wood were also sometimes used. But war and building projects, such as dams, have marred or threatened ancient sites.

The Mesopotamians built huge ziggurats, stepped pyramids that served as temples. The most famous of these mud-brick structures is the ziggurat of Ur, a three-tiered pyramid built by King Ur-Namu around 2300 B.C. and reengineered by Babylonian king Nebuchadrezzar II (605 to 562 B.C.). Another important architectural treasure from the time of Nebuchadrezzar II is the main gate of Babylon, which rests in a museum. Saddam Hussein ordered the rebuilding of this ancient city, which has been in progress since 1978.

Handcrafted in A.D. 1515, elaborate tiles decorate the walls and minaret of this shrine in Baghdad. **Islamic architecture** and art feature distinctive geometric patterns and floral designs.

After the Islamic conquest of Mesopotamia in the seventh century A.D., religious architecture became important. Because the Quran forbids the use of human figures in decorations, Islamic art focuses on geometric patterns and floral designs. The mosaic tile work of mosques (Islamic houses of worship) and the ornately hand-lettered prayers from the Quran present a stunning variety of styles and shapes.

Famous Islamic shrines include the al-Qadiriya in Baghdad, originally built as a religious school in the fourteenth century. The shrine's mosque has undergone several construction stages, including the addition of a dome in 1534 and a clock tower in 1898. The Younis Mosque in Mosul is also an important example of Iraqi Islamic architecture.

An extensive renovation, designed to modernize the site and better manage the crowds of pilgrims who visit each year, started in 1989.

Music

Music, especially folk music, is an important form of artistic expression in Iraq. Played on traditional instruments—such as the *oud* (an Arabian lute) and the *rebab* (a violin)—Iraqi music often accompanies the celebration of important events. Drums and chants are also part of Iraqi celebrations. Other traditional instruments are the *djooza* (four-stringed fiddle), the *santur* (drumsticks), the *rigg* (tambourine), and the *naggara* (metal shells beaten with metal sticks).

The *magam* is an important Iraqi musical genre that originated in Baghdad. Small groups of magam musicians perform on traditional instruments. The songs, led by singers called *qaari,* are popular in cities such as Baghdad and Mosul. One of the most popular modern groups is the Iraqi Magam Ensemble, founded in 1989 and led by singer Farida.

Many people in urban areas enjoy European classical music, and Radio Baghdad plays popular Western tunes. Iraq's most popular radio station, Voice of Youth FM, plays music from popular Western artists.

Strumming an **oud**, a kind of lute, this Iraqi musician performs a traditional song. Craftspeople make fine ouds by hand.

On the Islamic holiday of **Eid al-Adha,** or Feast of the Sacrifice, these children and parents are enjoying a day of vacation. The holy holiday takes a more serious tone when many followers sacrifice lambs to Allah.

Many older Iraqis prefer to hear traditional musical forms and instruments rather than modern music.

Holidays and Festivals

Before the 2003 conflict, Iraq marked various national holidays celebrating dates in the republic's history. Though it remains to be seen what will happen to national holidays in postwar Iraq, the Governing Council has banned six national holidays. These holidays were established under the Hussein government. In addition, the council declared April 9 a new national holiday, celebrating Iraqi liberation from the Hussein regime.

Most of Iraq's festivals mark religious holidays. The most important of these holidays is Ramadan, which takes place in the ninth month of the Islamic calendar. During Ramadan, people do not eat after sunrise or before sunset. They rise very early to eat a small breakfast, then gather for a small supper after dark.

At the end of Ramadan is the Eid al-Fitr, a three-day festival. Family and friends exchange cards and visit one another. They also give food and money to the poor. Children decorate their hands with henna (a reddish dye) and wear new clothes.

Other Islamic festivals include Eid al-Adha, or the Feast of the Sacrifice. This holiday is usually marked by the sacrifice of a lamb.

Muhammad's birth and death are also honored. Shiite Muslims celebrate the births and deaths of important imams.

Iraq's Kurdish population celebrates Nau Roy, or New Day. This festival takes place in the spring, around March 21. The celebration features parades, singing and dancing, picnics, and bonfires.

Food

Iraqi cuisine is rich and varied, ranging from kabobs (skewered chunks of grilled meat and vegetables) to *masgouf* (a specialty that includes fish from the Tigris River). Other popular dishes are *quzi* (stuffed roasted lamb) and *kubba* (minced meat, nuts, raisins, and spices).

Rice is a staple in Iraqi cooking. Most meals also include *samoons*, flat rounds of wheat bread. Arab coffee, which is brewed to be strong, thick, and bitter, is the nation's traditional drink. Tea served in small glasses is also popular. Desserts include fruit and baklava—a pastry made of honey and nuts layered between paper-thin sheets of dough.

Iraqis make lunch their main meal. It is usually served between 2 and 4 P.M. Supper usually consists of lunch leftovers and fruit.

CHICKPEA SOUP

Chickpeas (also known as garbanzo beans) are an important part of the Iraqi diet.

1 cup chickpeas

9 cups water

2 tablespoons butter

2 medium onions, diced

4 cloves garlic, crushed

½ cup fresh cilantro, finely chopped

½ teaspoon mustard powder

pinch of cayenne pepper

salt and pepper to taste

1. Soak chickpeas in water overnight. Drain and rinse.
2. Bring chickpeas and water to a boil. Cook over medium to low heat for 1½ hours.
3. In a separate pan, melt butter over medium heat. Add onions and garlic and heat until just brown. Add cilantro and heat for 2 to 3 minutes.
4. Add the butter mixture to the chickpeas. Add mustard powder, cayenne, and salt and pepper. Cover and cook over medium heat for 1 hour, or until chickpeas are tender.

Serves 6 to 8.

This merchant is tending to his **fruit and vegetable stand** at a Baghdad market. Times of war and economic sanctions have limited the availability and affordability of fruits and vegetables in Iraq.

Breakfast tends to be light, usually bread and jam. Before the 2003 war, Iraq was under economic sanctions, and few families could afford to buy many groceries. Most families relied on rice and bread as their main fare. In May 2003, the United Nations voted to lift the sanctions on Iraq, an action that allowed millions of dollars' worth of food to enter the country.

Sports and Recreation

Iraqis are enthusiastic sports fans. They especially love soccer, the country's most popular sport. Television stations air soccer matches played between the national league teams, and fans crowd the stadium in Baghdad. Basketball, volleyball, weight-lifting, horse racing, pigeon racing, and boxing are also popular sports.

Most professional Iraqi athletes are male, but the country has recently started a national women's soccer team. Many girls also play volleyball and tennis.

Iraq was once a center for athletics in the Middle East. But during the years that Hussein was in power, sports declined. Some of Iraq's Olympic athletes reported ongoing incidents of abuse and torture ordered by Uday Hussein. Many of these athletes left the country. Training facilities and stadiums in some areas of the country were limited and remain so. But Iraq hopes to build sports facilities and develop teams to compete at international sporting events.

A young **pigeon racer** proudly displays one of his fastest birds. Pigeon racing, enjoyed by Iraqi children and adults alike, involves releasing homing pigeons from a remote location and timing their return to their lofts.

An important part of Iraqi social life is visiting family and friends. People also go to movies, go to the theater, and watch television. Leisure time activities for Iraqi children include sewing, playing with dolls, and chess.

Television and reading are also popular pastimes. Before the 2003 war, the Iraqi government operated television and radio broadcasts. In postwar Iraq, television and radio stations are free from government control. People can also pick up foreign radio broadcasts. There are six major daily newspapers published in Iraq, one of which is in English. Communication systems have been modernized, and about 1 out of every 15 Iraqis owns a television set. Fewer people own computers. Radio remains the most popular communication system in Iraq.

Learn more about Iraqi cultural life at vgsbooks. com, where you'll find links to websites that feature various customs, recipes, holidays, music, art, literature, and more. Also find details on the ransacking of the National Museum in Baghdad.

THE ECONOMY

Money and investment are desperately needed in postwar Iraq. The downfall of the government has led to the near collapse of the Iraqi currency and to an inability to meet government payroll. Iraq's oil reserves are a potential resource to help fund the country's reconstruction, but sabotage and other problems have hampered oil sales.

The 2003 conflict led to crippling inflation, and Iraq's currency, the dinar, has been devalued and will be replaced by a new dinar in late 2003. During the 2003 war, it took nearly 4,000 dinars to equal one U.S. dollar. After the war, the rate has stabilized at about 2,000 dinars per dollar. Civil servants and those on government pensions have been hit the hardest by inflation. Some teachers in Iraq make as little as 3,500 dinars a month. They are forced to supplement their income with private lessons that hinder their ability to teach in the public schools.

On May 7, 2003, the United States lifted its embargoes on Iraq, allowing more humanitarian supplies to be sent to the country. For the first time in many years, Iraqis living in the United States are able to send

money to their relatives in Iraq. But those Iraqis without access to U.S. dollars, which are accepted as currency in postwar Iraq, are struggling.

Iraq has the resources to develop a strong, thriving economy. It sits on an estimated $3 trillion of untapped petroleum and has a well-trained and educated population. Many are optimistic about the economic future of Iraq, but this remains to be seen.

Oil and Mining

At the beginning of the twentieth century, Iraq's economy was predominantly agricultural. After oil was tapped in the 1920s, however, the country soon grew dependent on the oil industry. Between 1972 and 1975, the Iraqi government nationalized most of the country's oil resources and facilities. The Iraqi National Oil Company then assumed responsibility for exploration, production, transport, and marketing of crude oil and oil products. By the late 1980s, total crude oil exports had reached more than three million barrels per day.

OIL AND THE UNITED STATES

In the wake of the 2003 conflict, the United States is putting pressure on Iraqi oil workers to step up production on the country's most valuable resource. The money made from the sale of Iraqi oil is being placed in the Iraq Development Fund and will be used exclusively for reconstruction. Because of war-related damages and sabotage, Iraqi oil fields are returning to full capacity at a very slow rate.

A worker repairs piping at an Iraqi oil well following the 2003 war.

Before economic sanctions were imposed on Iraq in 1990, nearly all of the nation's oil was transported by pipeline through Turkey and Saudi Arabia.

Iraq has the second largest oil reserves in the world, after Saudi Arabia. Oil has traditionally provided nearly all of the nation's foreign income. The main oil fields lie in three regions—near Kirkuk, north-west of Mosul, and southwest of Basra.

In the mid-1990s, mining contributed less than 1 percent of the country's gross domestic product (GDP). The GDP is the amount of goods and services produced by the country in a year. In 1999 the UN authorized additional oil exports under the Oil-for-Food program to help provide humanitarian needs. This change raised the country's export revenues to almost 75 percent of prewar revenues. However, the UN Compensation Fund received 28 percent of these revenues to pay compensations to Kuwaiti war victims and to fund its own admin-istrative expenses.

After the 2003 war with U.S. and coalition forces, all remaining revenues from past oil sales and those from future sales have been deposited or will be deposited in an Iraqi development fund. Authorities have begun to spend the money on the rebuilding of Iraq. But funds have been more limited than projected, as sabotage and slow repair of oil wells and pipelines are hindering production and sale of Iraqi oil.

◉ Agriculture

Before the 2003 conflict, agriculture made up about 16 percent of Iraq's GDP and employed 11 percent of the country's workforce. Throughout Iraq's history, farmers have had to deal with seasonal droughts and floods. Because of unpredictable rainfall patterns, managing the rivers through canals and dams continues to be vital to successful farming. Nearly half of Iraq's land can be farmed, but only 13 percent of that amount is actually plowed and planted. Much territory lies unused each year to regain fertility, and a substantial portion of the remainder is pasture. Most food is imported from foreign countries. The amount of imported food has grown exponentially in Iraq since the end of international sanctions.

The country's most fertile farmland lies in the delta of the Tigris and Euphrates, where the rivers naturally water the land. In the Upper and Lower Plains, irrigation is essential to successful harvests. Iraq's most important crops include wheat, barley, corn, grapes, melons, oranges, and rice. In the northeast, where rainfall supplies enough water for crops, farmers grow barley, olives, tobacco, and fruit.

Farmers harvest **wheat** in northeastern Iraq prior to the 2003 war. Iraq cannot produce all the wheat it needs, so it must rely on imports of wheat and other grains. The 2003 war has further limited Iraq's agriculture.

The nation is one of the world's largest producers of dates, which flourish along the country's canals and rivers.

Although sheep dominate Iraq's domesticated herds, other livestock—such as cattle, horses, water buffalo, goats, and camels—are also raised. Most herding takes place in the northeast.

Agriculture has become exceedingly difficult in the aftermath of the 2003 war. Fields used for farming and herding have been bombed, have been flooded by malfunctioning pumps, and have been contaminated with cinders from burning oil fields. The movement of heavy vehicles has also degraded Iraq's farmland. A UN report in April 2003 declared the damages to Iraqi agriculture as part of an environmental crisis in the country.

Industry and Trade

The industrial sector has traditionally played a relatively small role in Iraq's economy. Manufacturing is underdeveloped and involves mostly refining oil and natural gas. Iraq also has factories that produce textiles, cement, and paper products. Other industrial work involves processing agricultural items, such as oil from vegetable seeds, flour from cereal grains, and leather from animal hides.

Iraq's cities, especially the capital, contain nearly all of the nation's manufacturing plants. After the Gulf War, all of the country's electrically powered facilities ceased functioning due to massive damage to power plants. The 2003 war caused similar problems, leaving many plants idle.

Because Iraq does not make many products, it must import most manufactured goods. The main imports are electrical machines, farming equipment, vehicles, and chemical products. After the 2003 war, Iraq desperately needed construction and electrical generation equipment to repair damages. International sanctions did not allow this type of machinery to be imported into Iraq. In May 2003, the UN passed a resolution lifting sanctions against Iraq, and the necessary machines became available.

LIFTING SANCTIONS

On May 22, 2003, the United Nations approved a resolution lifting economic sanctions against Iraq. The 2003 resolution allows for a great expansion of trade between Iraq and other nations. Iraq had been under UN sanctions for thirteen years. During this time, Iraq's economy suffered from a lack of foreign investment, and the standard of living for the Iraqi people was low. Many members of the UN are optimistic that the lifting of sanctions will improve the lives of Iraqis.

Forestry and Fishing

Less than .05 percent of Iraq is forested. Centuries of careless logging and land clearing have largely destroyed what once constituted Iraq's forests. The northeast, particularly around the border with Turkey, contains the largest areas of woodland. In these areas, stands of oak, maple, pistachio, hawthorn, and juniper trees grow. Much of the remaining woodlands provide wood for fuel and building materials.

Iraq's small fishing industry focuses on the country's river system and on several lakes. Most of the fish, therefore, consist of freshwater species, such as carp. Large catches come from the Tigris River. Most of the country's fishers use trawlers (a fishing boat) or small boats to haul in their catches. While fishing provides an important food source for the Iraqi people, it is not a significant export industry for Iraq.

During the 2003 war, many of Iraq's major waterways and freshwater sources did not receive proper maintenance. Military destruction released many hazardous substances into bodies of water throughout Iraq.

> **Rural fishers on the Euphrates still use traditional methods to make their catches. Because of the region's soaring temperatures, fishers usually go out at night in small boats. They drag huge, weighted nets, then row out against the river's current. At daylight they return to shore with their small boats filled with fish.**

These **fishers** are Madans, or Marsh Arabs. The haul caught in their nets will feed their families. Surplus fish can be sold to merchants.

The impact of this pollution on Iraqi fishing and wildlife preservation has yet to be fully investigated.

Energy and Transportation

Because of its vast oil reserves, most of Iraq's energy comes from oil-powered plants. Dams and hydropower stations, which have been built along the Tigris River and its tributaries, also generate electricity. Iraq has few dams, however, because the best dam sites on the Tigris lie in other countries.

Bombing raids during the Gulf War and the 2003 war heavily damaged energy facilities as well as road and rail networks throughout Iraq. Many regions must deal with electricity shortages, and travel is difficult in some areas.

Railways and highways link all of Iraq's major cities. About 1,500 miles (2,414 km) of railroad run within the country and also take passengers to Syria, Turkey, and Europe. When the system was built, however, builders used different track widths at different sections, making tracks impassable for trains within certain areas.

Iraq has an estimated 29,453 miles (47,400 km) of roads, and approximately 25,327 miles (40,760 km) of these are paved. These roads link Iraq's cities to each other and to neighboring countries. The most important highways run along the Syrian, Iranian, and Turkish borders. Cars and trucks use the roads between major Iraqi cities. In rural areas, camels, donkeys, and horses provide transportation.

The **port of Basra** serves large oceangoing vessels and small boats alike. Most of Iraq's oil is exported out of Basra. The Shatt al-Arab connects the port to the Persian Gulf, which lies 80 miles (129 km) to the south.

Visit vgsbooks.com for up-to-date information about Iraq's currency and economy.

Before the 2003 war, the Iraqi government owned the national airline, Iraqi Airways, which has airports at Baghdad, Bamerni, and Basra. International flights were virtually nonexistent, however, due to UN sanctions. With the lifting of sanctions in postwar Iraq, a small number of international flights have resumed to bring humanitarian supplies to the region.

Basra and Umm Qasr serve as commercial ports for oil tankers and other oceangoing vessels. River steamers can navigate the Tigris River between Basra and Baghdad.

The Future

Iraq's future remains uncertain. Since the end of the U.S.-led war in 2003, the country has been in the middle of an identity crisis. Decades of rule under Saddam Hussein and the Baath Party are over. Monuments and paintings of the leader have been torn down across the country, and books about Hussein have been removed from schools. The Iraqi people are moving toward a challenging new stage in the country's history.

Years of life under a dictator have left the Iraqi people ill equipped to create a democracy. Mistrust of outsiders and age-old conflicts between ethnic groups and political factions are making the initial transformation a formidable task.

Yet, progress is slowly being made. Humanitarian supplies have begun pouring into the country. Attempts to bring members of the Hussein government to justice for war and humanitarian crimes continue. While Hussein remains at large, several high-ranking officials have been taken into custody. Qusay and Uday Hussein, Hussein's sons and ranking members of their father's government, were killed during a U.S. raid in Mosul in July 2003. Deposed Vice President Taha Yassin Raman was captured the following month. Former exiles and representatives have come together to form a temporary government, the Governing Council. Members of the council have agreed to share the office of president of Iraq. The council also is working with U.S. authorities with the hope of holding free elections and writing a national constitution in the near future.

The people of Iraq have been through the terror of the Hussein regime and immense war-related struggles in the late twentieth century and early twenty-first century. Despite these great obstacles, the Iraqi people remain hopeful that their country can live in peace and prosperity in the years to come.

4000 B.C.	The city of Sumer is constructed in the Fertile Crescent (region of fertile land making up the Tigris and Euphrates River Valleys), leading to the rise of Sumerian city states.
c. 2300 B.C.	The ziggurat of Ur is constructed.
1900 B.C.	The Amorite Empire emerges.
1792–1750 B.C.	Hammurabi rules the city-state of Babylon and creates his legal code.
1570 B.C.	The Kassites take over Mesopotamia.
1116 B.C.	The Assyrian Empire reaches its greatest extent.
900–612 B.C.	The Assyrian Empire asserts a final expansion, conquering lands from the Mediterranean coast to modern northwest Iran, then collapses.
c. 500s B.C.	Nebuchadrezzar II refurbishes the ziggurat at Ur.
331 B.C.	Alexander the Great conquers Babylonia.
126 B.C.	The Parthians seize control of Mesopotamia.
A.D. 632	The prophet Muhammad, founder of Islam, dies.
600s	Islam spreads throughout Mesopotamia.
762	The Abbasids found the city of Baghdad.
1258	Mongol forces seize Baghdad.
1535	Mesopotamia becomes part of the Ottoman Empire.
1836	British steamboats travel up Mesopotamia's rivers.
1914	Mesopotamia fights against the Central Powers during World War I.
1921	The name Mesopotamia is changed to Iraq.
1922	Iraq becomes a British mandate, with the promise of independence in ten years.
1927	Oil is discovered at Kirkuk.
1932	Iraq becomes an independent kingdom.
1939	World War II breaks out. Iraq does not cooperate with Allied powers.
1941	British and Iraqi troops fight in Basra. Iraq is defeated.
1945	The Arab League is founded. Iraq joins the Arab League and the United Nations.

Timeline

1958   Iraqi forces, led by General Kassem and Colonel Arif, take over the government and declare Iraq a republic.

1963   Iraq adopts a national flag.

1968   The Baath Party assumes control of Iraq's government.

1972   Iraq nationalizes its oil industry.

1979   Saddam Hussein becomes president of Iraq.

1980   Iraq and Iran declare war against each other over territory disputes.

1981   "Land of Two Rivers" is adopted as Iraq's national anthem.

1988   The Iran-Iraq War ends with a cease-fire.

1989   Plans are introduced for the renovation of the Younis Mosque.

1990   Iraqi forces attack neighboring Kuwait, resulting in international criticism.

1991   After Iraq fails to withdraw from Kuwait, UN forces attack in a conflict known as the Gulf War.

1995   The UN launches its Oil-for-Food program to help starving Iraqi citizens.

2000   The United States adds Iraq to its lists of countries that sponsor terrorism.

2001   Following the September 11 terrorist attacks in the United States, Iraq falls under the suspicion of some members of the Bush administration for its possible involvement.

2002   U.S. president Bush names Iraq as a member of the "Axis of Evil." Tensions escalate between the United States and Iraq over Iraq's alleged weapons of mass destruction.

2003   The U.S. government sets a deadline for Iraq to comply with weapons inspections and demands that the Saddam Hussein government step down from power. Declaring that Iraq has failed to meet the deadline, the U.S government authorizes coalition forces to invade Iraq. They quickly gain control of the country, effectively ousting Saddam Hussein and the Baath Party from power. Attacks on U.S.-led coalition targets as well as UN and civilian sites continues. Hussein and other Baath Party members go into hiding. Search for Saddam Hussein, his sons, and other ranking members of the Hussein government begins. Several officials are captured immediately. Hussein's sons, Uday and Qusay, are killed during a raid in July, and former Iraqi vice president Taha Yassin Raman is captured in August. A terrorist bombing in August rocks Baghdad, destroying UN headquarters there.

COUNTRY NAME Republic of Iraq

AREA 169,236 square miles (438,319 sq. km.)

MAIN LANDFORMS Lower Plain, Syrian Desert, Upper Plain, Zagros Mountains

HIGHEST POINT Haji Ibrahim 11,811 feet (3,600 m) above sea level

LOWEST POINT Persian Gulf (sea level)

MAJOR RIVERS Diyala, Euphrates, Great Zab, Little Zab, Shatt al-Arab, Tigris

ANIMALS bats, camels, foxes, gazelles, jackals, sheep, wild pigs

CAPITAL CITY Baghdad

OTHER MAJOR CITIES Basra, Kirkuk, Mosul

OFFICIAL LANGUAGE Arabic

MONETARY UNIT Iraqi dinar, U.S. dollar. 1,000 fils = 1 dinar.

IRAQI CURRENCY

Iraq's official monetary unit has been the Iraqi dinar. Coins are available in 1, 5, 10, 25, 50, 100, and 250 fils. There are paper bills of 250, 500, and 1,000 fils. There are also notes of 1, 5, 10, 50, and 100 dinars. The value of the dinar has fluctuated wildly in postwar Iraq. Postwar plans include the stabilization of the Iraqi dinar and the printing of new banknotes based on the design of the old dinar. The new dinar will be issued in late 2003. Iraqis will be given a period in which they can exchange their old dinars for new dinar notes. The old notes will then become worthless. Once a freely elected government is in place, it will assume control of the Iraqi monetary system. U.S. dollars, which have historically been more stable than the dinar, are also recognized and used as official money in postwar Iraq.

Iraq's flag was adopted in 1963. The flag features three equal horizontal stripes of red, white, and black. The red symbolizes courage, the white stands for generosity, and the black represents Islamic triumphs. Three green stars and the takbir—the phrase *Allah Akbar*, or "Allah Is Great"—lie in the white stripe. The takbir was added to the flag during the Gulf War in 1991. It can be read from right to left on both sides of the flag. In 2003, the flag still flew over postwar Iraq. Reports suggest, however, that Iraqi leaders may decide to return to the pre-1991 flag.

The Iraqi national anthem, "*Ardulfurataini Watan*" ("Land of Two Rivers"), was adopted in 1981. The lyrics were written by Shafiq Abdul Jabar al-Kamali, and the music was composed by Walid Georges Gholmieh. The title refers to the Tigris and Euphrates Rivers, Iraq's two most important rivers, and the area where Baghdad, the capital city, is located. It is unknown whether the national anthem will change in postwar Iraq.

Land of Two Rivers
A home land that extended its wings over the horizon,
And wore the glory of civilization as a garment.
Blessed be the land of the two rivers,
A homeland of glorious determination and tolerance.

....

Oh expanse of glory, we have returned anew
To a nation that we build with unyielding determination.
And each martyr follows in the footsteps of a former martyr.
Our mighty nation is filled with pride and vigor
And the comrades build the fortresses of glory.
Oh Iraq, may you remain forever a refuge for all the Arabs
And be as suns that turn night into day!

 For a link to a site where you can listen to Iraq's national anthem, "Land of Two Rivers," visit vgsbooks.com.

FARIDA ALI (b. 1963) Farida Ali is a musician who was born in Karbala, Iraq. She is a popular singer who studied at the Institute of Music in Baghdad. Ali became the first woman in Iraq to specialize in and teach the classical style of music known as magam, which is traditionally sung by men. She performs with the Iraqi Magam Ensemble and has performed throughout the Arab world, Europe, and the United States. Her most recent work is contained on the CD *Mawal and Magamat.*

YOUSSIF ISMAEL AL-ANI (b. 1927) Youssif Ismael al-Ani is an Iraqi actor who was born in Baghdad. In 1952, after graduating from the Fine Arts Institute, he helped establish the country's Modern Theater Troupe. He also served as the head of the Modern Theater and the director of the Iraqi Center of Theater. Al-Ani has written and starred in three Iraqi films and has costarred in eight other Middle Eastern films. He has received many domestic and international awards for his work. He is considered a pioneer in modern Arab theater.

FAIK HASSAN (1914–1992) Faik Hassan was an Iraqi painter who studied art in Paris, France. After graduating in 1938, he returned to Iraq and created and directed the department of painting and sculpture at Baghdad's Institute of Fine Arts. He also established several artist groups, including the Pioneers Group in 1950 and the Corner Group in 1967. Throughout his career, he participated in many personal and group exhibitions, as well as most of Iraq's national exhibitions. His paintings are famous both at home and abroad. Hassan's works are characterized by their skillful painting techniques and their social and political subjects. One of Hassan's most famous works is the mural *Celebration of Victory*, which is located in Baghdad's Tiran Square. Hassan was born in Baghdad.

SADDAM HUSSEIN (b. 1937) Iraq's former president Saddam Hussein was born near Tikrit, Iraq, to a poor farm family. He grew up in a small village named al-Anja, northwest of Baghdad. When he was nineteen years old, Hussein joined the socialist Baath Party. His political ambitions led him to participate in a 1959 assassination attempt against Prime Minister Abdul Karim Kassem. After the attempt failed, Hussein was forced to flee to Syria and Egypt. In 1968 Hussein played a major role in the revolt that brought the Baath Party to power. He served as the country's vice president for eleven years, until President Hasan al-Bakr resigned in 1979. Hussein served as Iraq's leader until he was removed from power by U.S. and coalition forces in 2003. His current whereabouts are unknown.

A'ATIKAH AL-KHAZRAJY (1926–1997) A'atikah al-Khazrajy was a poet and writer born in the Diyala region. She wrote her first poem at age ten. She studied in the Arabic department at the Teacher's Institute. In 1956 al-Khazrajy became the first Iraqi woman to receive a doctorate from Paris's Sorbonne University. Her poetry is characterized by its romantic nature and involves themes such as nature and spiritual love. Her poetry collections include *Spirits of the Dawn* and *Layla's Madman.*

TAHA TAYH AL-NIAMEY (b. 1942) Taha Tayh al-Niamey is a scientist who serves as the secretary general of research councils, which works to develop scientific research. Born in Baghdad, al-Niamey obtained degrees from London University and Wales University. He served as chancellor of Baghdad University from 1981 to 1985 and has published many scientific essays as well as cultural and political works.

AHMAD AL-RADHI (b. 1964) Born in Samarra, Ahmad al-Radhi is an internationally known Iraqi soccer player who also coaches for one of the country's oldest professional soccer clubs. Before retiring from playing in 1997, al-Radhi played in many international matches, scoring 42 goals in 72 matches. In 1988 al-Radhi received the award for Asia Player of the Year. Throughout his career, he has coached Iraqi junior teams and has played for the country's professional clubs. Al-Radhi is considered one of the top ten Asian soccer players of the twentieth century.

JAWAD SALIM (1921–1961) Jawad Salim was an artist who was born to Iraqi parents living in Ankara, Turkey. As a young man, he studied art at schools in France, Italy, and Great Britain. He served as the head of the sculpture department at the Fine Arts Institute in Baghdad and, in 1951, established the Baghdad Group for Modern Art. His most famous work is his 1961 Monument to Liberty in Baghdad. After his death, Iraq's National Museum held an exhibition of his complete works.

WAFAA SALMAN (b. 1961) Wafaa Salman, a scholar and teacher who was born in Baghdad, moved to the United States in 1980 to study civil engineering at Boston's Northeastern University. After graduating in 1986, Salman established her own business, the Private Tutor, to tutor students in languages, science, and computers. She also returned to school to earn a political science degree in 1990. She has launched her own newsletter and radio programs covering events and workshops related to the Middle East and the Islamic world. She also established the Institute of Near Eastern and African Studies (INEAS) in Cambridge, Massachusetts.

IBRAHAM SALIH SHUKUR (1893–1944) Ibraham Salih Shukur, a writer born in Baghdad, is considered the father of Iraqi political writing. Shukur started his writing career at age seventeen, when he took a job as a journalist. Throughout his career, he published several newspapers, including *New Generation* and *Future,* which often criticized the government and its leaders. When the government restricted his publications, he continued his oppositional writing in letters to friends.

While Iraq is an interesting and beautiful country, instability still renders it a risky destination for tourists. Anyone considering going to Iraq should check with the U.S. State Department (see the department website at <http://travel.state.gov/ travel_warnings.html>) and with embassies in Iraq to determine the safety of travel in the region.

BAGHDAD Iraq's capital city is an ancient city as well as a modern commercial center. Steeped in history and culture, Baghdad houses many interesting museums and mosques. The Baghdad Museum offers visitors a view of Iraqi daily life through life-sized statues, and the Iraqi National Museum is the largest museum in the Middle East. The Iraqi National Museum covers Iraq's development from more than 100,000 years ago to the Islamic period. It was heavily damaged after the 2003 war but is being rebuilt and reorganized in postwar Iraq. Al-Khadhimain Mosque, one of the most important mosques in the Islamic world, is also here. The mosque was built in the sixteenth century on the site of two important religious shrines. Baghdad also boasts important modern sights, such as the Monument to Liberty and the Martyr's Monument.

BABYLON The ruins of the ancient city of Babylon lie 56 miles (90 km) south of Baghdad. One of the most famous and most beautiful cities of antiquity, Babylon was a cultural and political center renowned for its beauty and extravagance. Established about 1850 B.C., the city-state lasted until the 300s B.C. Remains of this city include the South Palace, which once housed the famed Hanging Gardens, the city's huge ziggurat, the impressive Ishtar Gate, and several temples.

CTESIPHON This ancient city near Baghdad was once the capital of the Parthian Empire starting around 129 B.C. and the Sassanian Empire starting in A.D. 226. The remains of a palace, built by the Sassanian king Chosroes I, still stand. The palace featured an 85-foot (26-m) vault, the largest arch recorded in ancient history.

KARBALA The city of Karbala is an important religious site for Shiite Muslims—second only to Mecca as a holy place for pilgrims. Karbala is the site of the mausoleum and shrine of al-Imam al-Hussein. Hussein was a Shiite leader who was killed in the city in 680. The tomb features a gilded dome, ten gates, and sixty-five rooms, all elaborately decorated. Many Shiite Muslims begin their pilgrimage to Mecca with a visit to Karbala.

AL-TAR CAVES This archaeological site lies south of Baghdad. It contains more than two thousand ancient artifacts related to the early Islamic age. Some of the antiquities found at the rocky caves include textiles and leather pieces.

Arabic: the official language of Iraq. Arabic has been used since the A.D. 600s and is one of the most widely used languages in the world.

cuneiform: wedge-shaped writing developed by the ancient Sumerians

delta: a triangular, fertile area of land where one or more rivers spread out into several outlets

Islam: a religion founded in the seventh century A.D. and based on the prophet Muhammad's teachings. Islam's holy book is the Quran.

mandate: a League of Nations commission given to a nation allowing that nation to administer a former German or Turkish territory after World War I

mosque: an Islamic place of worship

Muslim: a follower of Islam

nationalist: a person who feels supreme loyalty toward their nation and places a primary emphasis on the promotion of a national culture and national interests

Quran: the holy book of Islam. The writings in the Quran were set forth by the prophet Muhammad starting in 610. Muslims believe that Allah revealed these writings to Muhammad.

sanctions: trade restrictions limiting a country's imports and exports

shamal: a wind pattern that blows across Iraq from the north

sharki: an easterly wind that blows across Iraq

Shiite: a member of one of the two major Islamic sects. Shiites believe that only direct descendants of Muhammad are legitimate Islamic rulers.

Sunni: a member of one of the two major Islamic sects. Sunnis believe that Muhammad's successors can be chosen from among his closest colleagues and not necessarily from his direct relations.

Glossary

Background Notes. December 2001.
Website: <http://www.state.gov/r/pa/ei/bgn/> **(December 2, 2002).**
This site offers economic and historical information about Iraq.

Baghdad.com. December 11, 2002.
Website: <http://www.iraqdaily.com/> **(December 11, 2002).**
This site covers current events in Iraq, as well as information about the country's financial and economic sectors.

CountryWatch. December 2002.
Website: <http://www.countrywatch.com> **(December 2, 2002).**
CountryWatch includes information such as political history, economic conditions, environmental issues, and social customs in Iraq.

Europa Year World Book. Vol. 1. London: Europa Publications Ltd., 2001.
The article covering Iraq includes recent events, vital statistics, and economic information.

"Frequently Asked Questions Regarding New Iraqi Currency, July 7, 2003" *Usembassy.it.* July 7, 2003.
Website: <http://www.usembassy.it/file2003_07/alia/a3070706.htm> **(July 25, 2003).**
This website offers answers to questions about the new Iraqi currency slated for release in October 2003. Established to help Iraqis better understand the change, the site is a valuable resource for others as well.

Iraq Art and Culture. N.d.
Website: <http://i-cias.com/irq_art.htm> **(December 2, 2002).**
This website has information about the country's history and culture.

Iraq.net. December 2002.
Website: <http://www.iraq.net/> **(December 6, 2002).**
This website offers English-language news articles about current happenings in Iraq.

Lawler, Andrew. "Saving Iraq's Treasures." *Smithsonian*, No. 3 (June 2003): 42–55.
Lawler explores the Iraqi and international measures to preserve Iraq's archaeological, historic, and cultural treasures from war, looting, and progress of civilizaton. The essay features specific treatment of sites at Uruk, Ashur, Babylon, Hatra (al-Hadr), and Samarra.

Mance, Angelia L. *Iraq.* Philadelphia: Chelsea House Publishers, 2002.
Mance looks at Iraq's geography, history, and culture.

Oppel, Richard A., Jr. "Banking Overhaul and New Currency Planned for Iraq." *New York Times*, July 8, 2003.
Oppel covers the plan to revamp the banking system of postwar Iraq, including the pitfalls of freeing and stabilizing a banking system that has been under government control for more than twenty years.

Pincus, Walter, and Dana Priest. "Hussein's Sons Killed in U.S. Raid." *Washingtonpost.com.* **July 22, 2003.**
Website: <http://www.washingtonpost.com/> (July 22, 2002).
Pincus and Priest cover the U.S. raid on a Mosul home that resulted in a six-hour gunfight and ultimate death of Uday and Qusay Hussein.

Population Reference Bureau. **December 2002.**
Website: <http://www.prb.org> (December 2, 2002).
The bureau offers current population figures, vital statistics, land area, and more for Iraq.

Spencer, William. *Iraq: Old Land, New Nation in Conflict.* **Brookfield, CT: Twenty-First Century Books, 2000.**
This book focuses on Iraq's history, particularly the Iran-Iraq War and the Gulf War.

Statesman's Yearbook. **London: Macmillan, 2001.**
This resource features information about Iraq's historical events, industry and trade, and climate and topography, as well as suggestions for further reading.

Tyler, Patrick E. "Iraq's Council Steps Forward: It Abolishes a Holiday Marking Saddam's Rise." *New York Times.* **July 14, 2003.**
Tyler covers the formation of Iraq's first postwar government, it's deliberations, first decisions, and the issues with which it is confronted.

The World Factbook. **January 1, 2001.**
Website: <http://www.cia.gov/cia/publications/factbook/geos/ez.html> (November 30, 2002).
This website features up-to-date information about the people, land, economy, and government of Iraq. International issues are also briefly covered.

World Gazetteer. **February 15, 2002.**
Website: <http://www.gazetteer> (November 30, 2002).
The *World Gazetteer* offers population information about cities, towns, and other places in Iraq, including their administrative divisions.

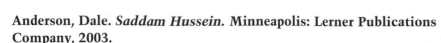

Anderson, Dale. *Saddam Hussein.* **Minneapolis: Lerner Publications Company, 2003.**
This biography covers the life of Iraq's controversial leader, including his rise to and fall from power.

ArabNet
Website: <http://www.arab.net>
This site covers the history and people of Iraq, including up-to-date news stories.

Corzine, Phyllis. *Iraq.* **San Diego: Lucent Books, 2003.**
This book looks at the government, land, and culture of Iraq.

Foster, Leila Merrell. *Iraq: Enchantment of the World.* **New York: Children's Press, 1998.**
Learn more about the people, history, and culture of Iraq.

———. *The Story of the Persian Gulf War.* **New York: Children's Press, 1991.**
This book discusses the causes and effects of the Gulf War.

Governments on the WWW: Iraq. **August 5, 2001.**
Website: <http:www.gksoft.com/govt/en/iq.html>
This website offers links to Iraqi political parties, news agencies, regional institutions, and more.

Kotapish, Dawn. *Daily Life in Ancient and Modern Baghdad.* **Minneapolis: Runestone Press, 2000.**
This book shows readers the evolution of Iraq's capital city from its ancient foundations to modern times.

Laird, Elizabeth. *Kiss the Dust.* **New York: Dutton Children's Books, 1992.**
In this novel for young readers, thirteen-year-old Tara is forced to flee her home in Iraq because of her family's involvement with the Kurdish resistance.

LoBaido, Anthony C., Yumi Ng, and Paul A. Rozario. *The Kurds of Asia.* **Minneapolis: Lerner Publications Company, 2003.**
Read about the history, cultural practices, economies, geograhic background, and struggles of the nomadic Kurds.

Losleben, Elizabeth. *The Bedouin of the Middle East.* **Minneapolis: Lerner Publications Company, 2003.**
Discover the culture, history, language, belief systems, migrations, religion, and adaptations of the Bedouin peoples of the Middle East.

McCaughrean, Geraldine. *One Thousand and One Arabian Nights.* **New York: Oxford University Press, 1999.**
This book is a modern translation of the classic collection of Arabian folktales. Join Scheherazade as she tells the tales of Sinbad, Ali Baba, and others.

Márquez, Herón. *George W. Bush.* **Minneapolis: Lerner Publications Company, 2002.**
Read about the life, times, and politics of the forty-third president of the United States.

Further Reading and Websites

Moss, Carol. *Science in Ancient Mesopotamia.* **New York: Franklin Watts, 1998.**
Discover the scientific achievements of the ancient Sumerians and Babylonians and how they contributed to modern science.

O'Connor, Karen. *A Kurdish Family.* **Minneapolis: Lerner Publications Company, 1996.**
This book covers the journey of a Kurdish family as they are forced to move from their home in Iraq to the United States.

Office of the Iraq Program Oil-for-Food. **August 6, 2003.**
Website: <http://www.un.org/Depts/oip/>
Learn more about the UN's Oil-for-Food program, including weekly updates.

Schaffer, David. *The Iran-Iraq War.* **San Diego: Lucent Books, 2002.**
Learn more about the Iran-Iraq War, including the reasons both nations waged the war and the outcomes for each.

Service, Pamela. *Mesopotamia.* **New York: Benchmark Books, 1999.**
This book looks at the history, achievements, and society of the ancient civilizations of Mesopotamia.

Taus-Bolstad, Stacy. *Iran in Pictures.* **Minneapolis: Lerner Publications Company, 2004.**
The author explores the history, government, religions, culture, and economy of Iran through text and photographs .

vgsbooks.com
Website: <http://www.vgsbooks.com>
Visit vgsbooks.com, the homepage of the Visual Geography Series®, which is updated regularly. You can get linked to all sorts of useful on-line information, including geographical, historical, demographic, cultural, and economic websites. The vgsbooks.com site is a great resource for late-breaking news and statistics.

Yeoman, John. *The Princes' Gifts: Magic Folktales from around the World.* **London: Pavilion Books, 1997.**
This collection of folklore includes tales from Iraq.

Zeman, Ludmila. *Gilgamesh the King.* **Toronto: Tundra Books, 1999.**
Zeman uses artwork to retell the *Epic of Gilgamesh*, the Sumerian masterpiece about a King Gilgamesh's quest for eternal life, for younger readers.

Captions for photos appearing on cover and chapter openers:

Cover: This is a reproduction of the Ishtar Gate, or Gate of Babylon. King Nebuchadrezzar II ordered the construction of the original gate in 575 B.C. One of eight gates in the impressive wall that surrounded Babylon, the gate was named for the Babylonian goddess Ishtar and served as the main entrance to the city. A reconstruction of the Ishtar Gate, built from the original bricks, currently is in a museum in Germany.

pp. 4–5 Bullet holes mar this mural of deposed Iraqi leader Saddam Hussein. Venting years of hidden anger over Hussein's cruelty, some Iraqi citizens defaced or destroyed images and statues of the leader following his fall from power.

pp. 8–9 Sand and sparse vegetation make up the arid landscape of southwestern Iraq. Trees cluster around a small area of freshwater in the background.

pp. 18–19 The ziggurat, or terraced and pyramid-shaped temple, withstands the forces of nature and time at the ancient Sumerian city of Ur. Religious scholars believe Ur to be the birthplace of Abraham, a key religious figure in the Islamic, Judaic, and Christian religions.

pp. 36–37 Iraqis shop for produce and other goods at an outdoor market in Baghdad. At Iraqi markets, many vendors provide goods to customers.

pp. 46–47 Muslims perform Friday prayers at an Iraqi mosque. Islam is the main religion in Iraq.

pp. 58–59 Rich with oil, Iraq has only a few ports suitable for the export of oil. Pipelines, such as this one, are used to move oil from oil fields to these ports.

Photo Acknowledgments

The images in this book are used with the permission of: Sahib/AFP/Getty Images, pp. 4-5; © Reuters NewMedia Inc./CORBIS, pp. 7, 33 (right); Ron Bell/Digital Cartographics, pp. 6, 11; © TRIP/J. Sweeney, pp. 8–9, 12, 17, 21, 50, 51 (right), 52, 64; © TRIP/ASK Images, pp. 10, 36–37, 58–59; © Vivian Ronay/ZUMA Press, p. 13; © AFP/CORBIS, pp. 14–15, 54, 60; © Husbands/ Royal Navy/ZUMA Press, p. 16; © David Lees/CORBIS, pp. 18–19; © Gianni Dagli Orti/CORBIS, p. 20; © Hulton|Archive by Getty Images, pp. 23, 31; © TRIP, p. 24, 27, 38 (right), 63; © Hulton-Deutsch Collection/CORBIS, pp. 26–27; © Bettmann/CORBIS, pp. 29, 49; © CORBIS, p. 32; © Isaac Menashe/ZUMA Press, p. 33 (left); © Stephanie Sinclair/CORBIS, p. 34; Mark Cator/Impact/ ZUMA Press, p. 38 (left); © Caroline Penn/PANOS Pictures, pp. 40, 46–47; © Patrick Andrade/UNICEF/ZUMA Press, p. 42; © Crown/ZUMA Press, p. 43; © Sgt. L. A. Salinas/DOD/ZUMA Press, p. 44; © Arlo Abrahamson/ U.S. Navy Photo/ZUMA Press, p. 48; © Abilio Lope/CORBIS, p. 51 (left); © Shepard Sherbell/CORBIS SABA, p. 53; © Giacomo Pirozzi/PANOS Pictures, pp. 56, 57; © Ed Kashi/CORBIS, p. 61.

Cover photo: © TRIP/J. Sweeney. Back cover photo: NASA.